Peyton

1/15,

D0055742

Mutual Ministry

Mutual Ministry

NEW VITALITY FOR THE
LOCAL CHURCH

James C. Fenhagen

THE SEABURY PRESS · NEW YORK

The Seabury Press
815 Second Avenue
New York, N.Y. 10017

Quotations from the Holy Scriptures are from The New English Bible,
copyright 1961, 1970 by the
Delegates of the Oxford University Press
and the Syndics of the Cambridge University Press.

Copyright © 1977 by The Seabury Press, Inc.

All rights reserved.
No part of this book may be reproduced,
stored in a retrieval system, or transmitted, in any form or by any means,
electronic, mechanical, photocopying, recording, or otherwise,
without the written permission of The Seabury Press.

Printed in the United States of America

Library of Congress Cataloging In Publication Data

Fenhagen, James C   Mutual ministry.
1. Pastoral theology. 2. Church. I. Title.
BV4011.F45   253'.2   76-49997   ISBN 0-8164-0332-5

Sixth Printing

For Eulalie,
companion in marriage
and fellow journeyer
from whom I have learned much
about what it means to love and to grow.

Contents

Mutual Ministry

Introduction

Several years ago the British journalist, Monica Furlong, published a little book entitled *With Love to the Church*, which, as the title suggests, paid tribute to the life-giving qualities which the Christian Church has given to the world down through the centuries. In many ways this book is an echo of Monica Furlong's affirmation. It seeks to affirm the life-giving qualities of the local congregation in a way that brings into focus new possibilities for the future. My point of view has been shaped by my encounter with Holy Scripture, by what I have learned from the behavioral sciences, and from my own experience as an educator and parish priest.

In the spring of 1975 I happened to be in Baltimore, Maryland, the city where I had grown up. I had gone there to have lunch with my brother, but since I arrived half an hour early, I decided to walk over to St. Paul's, the old downtown church that had been my parish. I went inside and sat down. The church was lighted but empty. As I sat there, I was suddenly overwhelmed by memories. For an instant I was a little boy singing in the choir, and then an acolyte who fainted from kneeling so long on Easter Sunday. I recalled the feeling of terror standing in that great pulpit as a young seminarian on Theological Education Sunday, the excitement of my ordination, and the terrible sadness during my mother's funeral—all of which took place in this old church. I had not been particularly active in the church as a young person for any length of time but sitting there that morning I realized how, in so many ways, this institution had touched my life. I do not think I am particularly romantic about the local church. Like many people I have been very often bored to death, and as a pastor I have obviously contributed to the boredom of others. I have wept over the church's resistance to change and its hesitancy to seize new opportunities. But nevertheless I can affirm the church. I can affirm it as a life-giving institution without which society would be profoundly bereft. I can affirm the local church because of what I have experienced in my own life and what I have seen in the lives of others.

This book is written for those persons in the local church —clergy and laity—who are concerned about the vitality of the congregations to which they belong. It is based on the assumption that if you are going to address the issue of congregational vitality with any real seriousness, you must look at four elements: the vision by which the church lives; the ministry through which the church acts; the structures by which the church is shaped; and the experience of faith in which the church is nourished. Chapters I and IX, the first and last, are concerned primarily with the question of vision—what the local church might be now and what it is called to be in the future. Chapters II through VI concentrate on the ministry of the church and the experience of faith. In Chapter II, I describe briefly some possible functions of ministry needed in today's world. Then in the four chapters that follow, Chapters III through VI, I take each of these functions and develop them more fully. In Chapters VII and VIII, with this understanding of ministry in mind, I then turn to the question of structure. How do we organize a congregation for a more mutual ministry, and how, in particular, can the pastor be given the training and support he or she needs to help bring this about?

A provocative monologue by Binx Bolling in Walker Percy's novel, *The Moviegoer,* touches what seems to me to be the nerve of our quest for vitality and meaning. The monologue has to do with that undefined, often inarticulated search that seems to drive us to look beneath the surface of things. As Binx states it: "What is the nature of the search? you ask. Really it is very simple, at least for a fellow like me; so simple that it is easily overlooked. The search is what anyone would undertake if he were not sunk in the everydayness of his own life. This morning, for example, I felt as if I had come to myself on a strange island. And what does such a castaway do? Why, he pokes around the neighborhood and he doesn't miss a trick. . . . To become aware of the possibility of the search is to be on to something. Not to be on to something is to be in despair."[1]

Discouragement, indeed despair, settles upon a congregation when it gives up searching for new possibilities. As Binx Bolling says, "To become aware of the possibilities of the search is to be on to something." A vital congregation is a congregation constantly engaged in the search for new possibilities. It is hoped that this book will provide some new windows from which light might come to illumine the search in which we are all engaged. They are offered "with love to the church."

Much of what follows, although disguised, is personal. I am indebted, therefore, to the many people from whom I have learned: to the people of St. Paul's and Holy Nativity churches in Baltimore; St. Mark's Parish, Frederick County, Maryland; St. Michael and All Angels' Church, Columbia, South Carolina; the churches of the Diocese of Washington; and to the people of St. John's Church, Georgetown Parish in Washington, D. C. I am grateful for my colleagues at the Hartford Seminary Foundation and to my good friend, Earl Brill of the College of Preachers in Washington, D.C. They have taken the time to read what I have written and to offer their suggestions. I have tried where possible to eliminate sexist language, but admittedly have not always been successful. Finally, I am especially indebted to Audrey Ermakovich and Micki Smith who have critiqued, typed and retyped what has now become "our book."

CHAPTER I

The Local Church
and a Changing World Order

. . . the old order has gone, and a
new order has already begun.

2 CORINTHIANS 5:17

I

What we often see in the life of a typical Christian congregation is but the tip of the iceberg. What lies beneath the surface
is what has brought people back week after week, century
after century. For one person it was something that happened
as people reached out to her at the time of the death of her
child. For another person, it was the time on a weekend conference when life suddenly began to fit together. Other people
might speak of an experience of worship, or of a social action
project, or of the time when someone spoke the name of Christ
in a way that touched something very deep within them. All
these experiences are integral to the life of a Christian congregation, but they are the things that you do not see unless you
look beneath the surface. The Christian faith for most people
is not communicated by doctrinal pronouncements or the sol-
emn assembly of ecclesiastical dignitaries, but by what goes on
in the church in its most local setting. It is here, in the church
down the street, that people are caught up in the Gospel promise—or are turned away. It is the conviction underlying this
book that the parish church, despite its often glaring inadequa-

cies, is in a unique position to help men and women move into a new world with courage and hope.

We stand today on the edge of a new order. No one knows for sure what is before us, but we do know that it will be vastly different from what we have known in the past. Robert Heilbroner speaks of the inevitability of what he calls "convulsive change"; change forced upon us by external events rather than by conscious choice, "by catastrophy rather than by calculation."[1] By now the catalogue of dilemmas facing the modern world are household expressions—overpopulation, depletion of our natural resources, environmental pollution, the increasing gap between the "haves" and the "have nots"—but it is difficult to accept the fact that our conventional approaches to these problems are no longer effective. We have come to the end of an era. The need for change touches the very attitudes we hold and the style in which we are accustomed to live. For most of us, however, the resistance is high. Despite all that we affirm and profess to believe, there is something inside of us that holds on desperately to the irrational conviction that if we go about business as usual and keep calm, someone somewhere will figure out the solution. As Douglas Hall so aptly points out: "We want a world in which problems are soluble—chiefly by technological means. We want to believe *ourselves* to be the bearers of the solution, of salvation!"[2]

The local congregation is of crucial importance to modern life because what we really face in contemporary society is a theological problem of mammoth proportions. The gods of technology have proved less than divine. What we will need to survive is not a new plan or a new ideology but the inner resources necessary for facing a profound crisis of faith. The Christian Gospel offers such inner resources—resources that emerge out of the conviction that the hope of the world lies not in man's technological genius but in the creative energy of God. It is not that we do not work for ways of resolving the stupendous problems that face humankind. It is rather that we do so with humility that keeps us open to the need and possibility of divine grace. Apart from this, we are in bondage to a view of human existence that raises the desire for power and control to demonic proportions. Our hope lies not in our ability to save ourselves but in the power of God to bring life out of death.

The Christian message is an invitation to participate in a new dimension of life, a dimension built on the ashes of human destructiveness and greed. It is in the face-to-face encounter with this reality that the need to control is transformed into the ability to love. Love is a gift. It can never be demanded or bought or controlled. It is the life-giving energy of God, out of which a sense of responsibility for the world emerges—a responsibility based, not on human arrogance and pride but on the belief that God is indeed at work in his world—healing, transforming, creating life in the midst of death. "Behold! I make all things new! . . . I am the Alpha and the Omega, the beginning and the end" (Rev 21:5, 6).

The central conviction underlying this book is that the local congregation of the Christian Church is uniquely equipped to enable persons to face the world of tomorrow (indeed of today), not as part of the problem (which it often is) but as a participant in what will ultimately be God's solution. This uniqueness is based, not on any particular skills we possess but on the power of the message we proclaim. Questions of meaning, of value, of compassion, and of faith are fundamental questions that confront everyone at some level of their existence. It is the response to these concerns that is the primary business of the Christian Church at every level, no matter what its size or persuasion.

I am well aware that in many instances the local church is ill-prepared to deal with such questions. I am aware that in some congregations, the experience of "death" is seemingly stronger than the experience of "life." The question, however, is not an either/or question. The local church is like any gathering of people that has begun to take institutional form. The Christian Church is a combination of opposites. Our task is not to reach perfection but to so structure our common life that the forces of life are enhanced and the forces of death diminished. The forces of life are those combinations of experiences—sometimes quite intentional, sometimes quite spontaneous—that release human creativity and produce growth. Life experiences have a way of linking us up with those deep places within ourselves, and then turning us outward. In theological language, life experiences are experiences of the kingdom of God—those moments when we are most open to the movement of the Spirit in ourselves and in others around us.

II

Anyone who has ever been through the process of choosing a congregation knows something of what it means to identify the life-giving forces that are at work. Although our criteria are sometimes different, our intent—unless of course we are in psychological flight—is the same. We are looking for an experience that activates the life forces within us, an experience that makes us feel better for having participated in it. Several years ago, it was my good fortune to encounter a remarkable family—a mother and four daughters—who went about the process of choosing a church with beautiful precision. They began by listing all the things they wanted in a church—sermons that touched them personally, a congregation that sings, an authentic friendliness. They agreed on their top ten priorities, and then they began visiting churches on Sunday mornings, each with their own score card. After visiting five or six congregations, they shared their ratings. The church that received the highest common rating in each of their categories became their choice, the congregation to which they then made a serious commitment.

We all have criteria by which we measure the forces of life in a congregation. Even if these criteria are never articulated, they are nevertheless there, shaping the nature of our expectations and the degree of our commitment. Since this book is about the local church, what follows obviously is based on the criteria I hold up as signs of life. At this particular moment in my life, seven of these criteria seem of special importance. I do not pretend that they are the last word or that they are necessarily exhaustive. I do know that when I search for signs of life and vitality within the Christian community, these are some of the things I look for:

1) Life is enhanced when a congregation takes seriously the communication of its biblical and theological tradition.

No Christian congregation exists in and of itself. We are a people who have been and who continue to be formed by a story. Jesus told his disciples: "Heaven and earth will pass away; my words will never pass away" (Mk 13:31). Ours is a story whose words are empowered by *the* Word. It is a story that begins at the world's creation; climaxes in the life, death, and resurrection of Jesus Christ; and propels us into the future as a people who have experienced a new order of human existence. "And be assured, I am with you always, to the end of time" (Mt 28:20).

Every group of Christians will find a way of communicating this story according to the gifts they have been given. Indications of their seriousness will be seen in a way in which the Scriptures are read in worship, or made use of as part of the ongoing life of the congregation. It will involve opportunities for serious theological reflection upon the issues facing every aspect of the created order. A sign of life for me would be whether or not I was being drawn into the story in a way which opened me to the mystery of life, as opposed to having the story "laid on" in such a way that I was cut off from the great questions that surround my existence.

The task of the congregation is not to give people certainty but to deepen faith. In faith I can live with the ambiguities of life without having to wear blinders. Religious truth is normal experience understood at full depth. To be caught up in the story of redemption is to be transformed from within, engaged in a quest, knowing who we are and to whom we belong. I look to the local congregation to help me live into the Gospel in such a way that this quest is nourished in continuous dialogue with a world full of both pain and promise.

2) Life is enhanced when a congregation works at building and sustaining authentic community.

Community is not something we create. It is a gift, a mark of the Spirit. On the day of Pentecost, a gathering of people became a living community. We read in Acts of the Apostles: "The whole body of believers was united in heart and soul. Not a man of them claimed any of his possessions as his own, but everything was held in common, while the apostles bore witness with great power to the resurrection of the Lord Jesus" (Acts 4:32–33). This first Christian congregation was drawn together by the power of the Holy Spirit with several clearly distinguishable characteristics. There was a degree of openness among them that not only resulted in a willingness to share their possessions and their particular gifts, but that drove them to bear witness to their experience in the world at large. Christian community is never anything static. It is a rhythm in which we experience both intimacy and separateness, nurture and mission.

A sign of authentic community would be the degree of trust that seems to exist in the congregation, a trust exhibited in such things as the way people deal with conflict or in the opportunities that exist for personal sharing and support. Another and particularly critical sign would be seen in the way a congregation structures its common life—the degree of mutuality that exists between the ordained and other members of the community, or the way in which people's differing gifts are identified and made use of. There are many Christian congregations in which it is very difficult to experience genuine community. Relationships have been ritualized to the point where authentic encounter is almost impossible to achieve. Well established and often hierarchical patterns of decision making keep individual gifts well hidden and creativity under control. There are some congregations that are so structured, so governed by custom, that it is a wonder community occurs at all. And yet, almost despite us, it does. The Spirit will not be bound. We are called into community sometimes over our strongest objections. It is a mark of authentic life when a congregation can identify the points at which this begins to happen and, with patience and care, nurture what God has begun.

3) A critical sign of life for a congregation today would be the capacity to help people take upon themselves the discipline necessary for authentic personal and spiritual growth.

In *New Seeds of Contemplation*, Thomas Merton writes: "Our vocation is not simply to *be*, but to work together with God in the creation of our own life, our own identity, our own destiny—to work out our own identity in God, which the Bible calls 'working out salvation,' is a labor that requires sacrifice and anguish, risk and many tears. It demands close attention to reality at every moment, and great fidelity to God as He reveals Himself, obscurely, in the mystery of each new situation."[3]

The changes being demanded of us are almost beyond com-

prehension. For vast numbers of people living in the West—
the world of the "haves"—it will mean a total reorientation of
life-styles. It will mean learning how to resist the urge to buy
and the urge to eat, where submitting to those urges is our
custom. It will mean discovering the simplicity which comes
from an intentional life lived from inside out rather than from
outside in. In the riches of the Christian tradition there are
patterns for this kind of pursuit, easily adapted to present
needs. To adopt them, however, will require not only assistance but ongoing support.

In her helpful study entitled *Religious Pilgrimage,* Jean Haldane makes this comment: "Perhaps in our generation, in a
culture that is individualistic and puts a value on personal
growth and understanding, the Church's primary task is to
help people with this important work of integrating past experience and delving deeper within themselves for that 'underground stream' of spiritual unity with others and with God."[4]
A serious response to this task on the part of any congregation
is a vital sign of spiritual growth and life.

*4) Life is enhanced when there is a clear and organized response to
the redemptive activity of God in the world at large.*

"The religious suppose that only the religious know about
God, or care about God, and that God cares only for the
religious." So wrote William Stringfellow in 1962, words that
still cast a shadow over institutionalized religion. "The
church," he continues, "is not the place where men come to
seek God; on the contrary, the church is just the place where
men gather to declare that God takes the initiative in seeking
men. The church, unlike any religion, exists to present to the
world, and to celebrate in the world, and on behalf of the
world, God's presence and power and utterance and action in
the on-going life of the world."[5]

If a congregation believes this, it will mean that it expends as much energy engaging the world in which it is immersed as it does on the nurturing of its common life. Ministries of caring, ministries on behalf of justice and reconciliation, ministries of witness, ministries of dialogue, ministries that bring Christian values to bear in the decision-making process of politics and business, ministries of support—all potentially stem from the local congregation, and when carried out with wisdom and compassion are signs of life. The congregation *is* mission. The congregation is also evangelistic. Both are essential to its very nature. In looking for signs of life I find myself immediately looking for how this sense of mission is being expressed, and by whom. Mission, be it explicit or implicit, is the primary task of the laity. It is a task that requires training and support, a task that is essential as we confront the chaos of a world faced with cataclysmic change.

Mission is the response of the people of God to the reconciling work of Christ in the world. As Paul so eloquently attests: "From first to last, this has been the work of God. He has reconciled us men to himself through Christ, and he has enlisted us in this service of reconciliation" (2 Cor. 5:18). Mission then, is not as much a program as it is a process, a way of life. It can be seen in a group of persons meeting weekly at lunch hour for Bible study and reflection on the decisions that confront them. It can be seen in a highly disciplined parish task force organized to address a particular community problem. It can be seen in the cooperative efforts of local churches, or of the whole Christian Church with community agencies to bring about a more humane world. It can be seen in a congregation's support of a special ministry nearby or in another part of the world. It can be seen in the witness of one person to another or to the life-giving power of the Gospel. Mission is not something a congregation takes on when all the bills are paid. It is at the heart of what it means to be the church. "The church is to mission," someone once wrote, "as fire is to burning." The spirit of mission within a congregation is therefore a critical sign of life.

5) Life is enhanced when caring for persons is viewed and acted upon as the work of the congregation at large.

One of the great heresies of the contemporary church is the idea that the primary role of the ordained person in a congregation is to exercise a ministry of caring on behalf of the others who are responsible for his or her hire. For awhile this heresy was so rampant that the mark of a successful ministry was seen in the number of people who came for counseling. Such a view is heretical because it institutionalizes and delegates the ministry of caring to one or two individuals rather than to the congregation at large. The sign of a congregation's capacity to care is not seen in the sensitivity of the clergy, but in the number of people who are being trained and supported in caring for one another.

As the recession began to take its toll and layoffs occurred, one congregation gathered persons who were particularly qualified to help others who were out of work. Another congregation developed a training program called "Helping Helpers to Help." Out of this, divorced persons were able to bring assistance to persons going through the pain of divorce. Persons who had come to terms with grief in their own lives were able to provide support for those confronted by death. In another congregation, a group of men organized themselves to act as father substitutes for children without fathers. Another congregation developed a disciplined visitation program to hospitals, shut-ins, and people just in need of company.

One of the devastating effects of mass communication is overexposure to pain and suffering. We are inundated with human tragedy. Since there is no way we can respond to all that we see, we begin to build defenses against our own feelings of helplessness and horror. Unless there is some way in which we can act, we find ourselves becoming apathetic and detached. It could well be that the greatest threat to human survival is not the loss of energy or the shortage of food but the loss of compassion.

A local congregation is uniquely equipped to help deepen our capacity for caring. Its willingness and ability to do this is a mark of life. In no way does this diminish the skills of the ordained or of others who bring particular professional know-how to the task. It merely places the burden of caring on all who live in the Lord's name, that they, as the Gospel states, might "fulfill the law of Christ."

6) Life is enhanced when an educational environment is created which exhibits in practice what is said in word.

The educational task of the local congregation has but one aim: To help men, women, and children grow as whole persons in their response to the Gospel of Jesus Christ. Education then is a process. It is carried on by a combination of relationships, structural and organizational arrangements, programs and gatherings for worship, and interpersonal exchange, all of which combine to teach what this particular group of people understand the Christian Gospel to be about. Where spontaneity and self-expression are encouraged, we are teaching something about the kinds of persons God created us to be. When relationships between people are formal and distant, we are teaching what we believe about Christian community, regardless of what we read or say to the contrary. A sign of life, then, in the educational process of a congregation, is the attempt on the part of a significant number of persons to bring into harmony what is said with what is done. The way the church is organized, its governance, as well as the content and structure of its program, are educational issues.

The churches that are able to provide a life-giving educational experience for children are those who are equally concerned about the ongoing growth of adults. Again, it's a matter of practicing what we preach. If there is no challenge to adults to take their own growth seriously, then the environment necessary for a total educational emphasis will be diminished. Growth involves more than passive receptivity. Growth involves the internalization of new ideas, attitudes, and feelings. For this to occur, there must be regular opportunities for interpersonal sharing, opportunities to wrestle and question, opportunities to encounter the mystery of another human being, opportunities that call forth our emotions and inspire us with new possibilities.

A congregation in Washington, D.C., has a six-month program which prepares people for participation in Christian community. A mark of belonging to that congregation is participation in that class, and then taking the responsibility for recruiting and teaching others. An environment has been established that is conducive to growth. Small group experiences, weekend conferences, variety in method and style, are all signs of life—ways in which we enter into the story of redemption from the inside out, rather than only from outside in. Henri Nouwen writes: "If education is meant to challenge the world, it is Christ himself who challenges teachers as well as students [and we are both] to give up their defenses and to become available for real growth. . . . We might be thrown from our horses and blind for a while, but in the end we will be brought to an entirely new insight, which might well bring about a new man in a new world."[6]

7) Life is enhanced when the experience of worship is able to gather up feelings of belonging, celebration, and awe and offer them to the glory of God.

The vitality of worship is the sine qua non of congregational life. If all the church ever did together was to gather for worship, it would be responding to him who is the very essence of life. As Paul Hoon has written, "The world may indeed set the church's agenda, as we are fond of saying, but it is God who in the Event of Jesus Christ has called the meeting. In her worship uniquely, the church again and again hears that call."[7] The tragedy, however, is that the nature of this worship too often reveals "less the joyful song of the 'new man' than the tiresome and familiar refrain of the old captivity in which nothing has been made new."[8]

On a given Sunday, a congregation at worship is made up of many different people at different points on the spectrum of life experiences. What touches and involves one person may bypass another completely. Although worship is by definition God-centered, it is an act offered by the entire Christian community. The test of vitality and life, therefore, involves the degree and the way each member of the community is enabled to participate. This suggests, not only participation in the act of worship itself but in the planning as well, as far as this is appropriate and possible.

The key to vitality in worship, of course, is our openness to the Spirit. Such openness can be enhanced when we become intentional about what we do. Worship is a dramatic reenactment of the story that has called us into being. Every word, every gesture, every offering of music, every prayer needs to be seen in terms of what it is we expect could happen. When the Bible is read in a monotone, followed immediately by a prayer or a hymn (leaving no time for silent reflection), how do we expect people to be drawn into the story that we are proclaiming? What can we do to enhance the experience of community, of personal reflection, of awe, and of wonder as we gather to celebrate God's presence in the world?

I have often wondered why we have not made better use of the musical talent in our communities to enhance the aesthetic quality of our worship—violinists, trumpeters, flutists, to name but a few. We might even consider installing stereo equipment in some smaller churches. In this way, the congregation might experience some of the great music of its tradition, especially where the music budget is limited. The same thing, of course, could be said for visual presentation. The experience of worship involves the whole person—body, mind, and spirit. When a congregation becomes intentional about what it is doing and what it needs to do, there is the experience of vitality and life.

William Abernathy, in *A New Look for Sunday Morning*, describes how one congregation became intentional about its worship:

Our effort centers around the development of a three-part Sunday morning program of worship, education, and celebration. The transition of South Church from a church where the adults gathered each Sunday from eleven to twelve o'clock to sit stoically in their places in order to be "ministered to" to a church where members of all ages sit together, where people can feel free if they wish to take part vocally in a corporate prayer, where occasional applause and laughter can be heard, and where in a worshipful atmosphere we minister with each other—this is a strange and wonderful transition.[9]

Numerous other congregations have become intentional about worship in their own way. The form is not half as important as the participation and the intent. When worship is a priority in the life of a congregation, there is life.

III

The world of tomorrow will be very different from the world of today. We stand on the edge of a new time. Two thousand years ago, however, the Christian Church found itself in a similar position. The patterns of Greco-Roman culture, which had held the world together for so long, were beginning to show cracks at the seams. Values were changing as the old ways of viewing things began to pass away. It was this world in which the Christian community was born. It has survived because, by the grace of God, it offered—even in its most accommodating moments—a different way.

This book is about that community—the Christian Church —as it lives out its life today on the local level. It is about ministry in all of its varied forms. It is about the way we exercise ministry in the world in which we live, as well as the way we minister to one another. The emphasis is not so much on radical change—although this is often needed—as it is on finding ways to free the church to be what by calling it is. Our task is to find ways of releasing the gift each of us has been given, in order that we might enter more fully into the creative purpose of God. The place to begin, then, is with the ministry of the Christian Church—a ministry not limited to the ordained but given to all who bear allegiance to Jesus Christ.

No congregation has fully developed the ministry available to it. It is here, however, that the seeds of renewal are present. Our concern, then, is in working with what is in order to find ways that we might be contributors to what is emerging, rather than being caught as part of the problem. We boast of no overnight solution, but we do stand open to be transformed by him who is the Alpha and the Omega, the beginning and the end.

CHAPTER II

Toward a More Mutual Ministry

> *John said to him, "Master, we saw a man driving*
> *out devils in your name, and as he was not one of*
> *us, we tried to stop him." Jesus said, "Do not stop*
> *him; no one who does a work of divine power in my*
> *name will be able the next moment to speak evil*
> *of me. For he who is not against us is on our side."*
>
> MARK 9:38–40

I

Ministry is a special word within the Christian Church. It comes from the Greek word *diaconos,* meaning "one who serves." It refers primarily not to a special office (the ordained ministry) but to a special function. The New Testament is quite clear about this. Ministry is an act undertaken in the name of Christ. " 'In your name, Lord,' they said, 'even the devils submit to us' " (Lk 10:17), a theme reflected in the passage from St. Mark's Gospel quoted above. The point is that ministry is more than simply doing good. Ministry is an act performed *in his name.* Therefore, it is not something we do solely on our own, but something Christ does in us, through us, and with us. Ministry has been given to us. Our task is to uncover what is already present so that the ministry of the church might be carried out in all of its fullness. The ministry of the church is exercised by every man, woman, and child who bears the mark of baptism.

Whenever you talk about the ministry of the Christian community, however, you are talking about a particular view of the church, and views obviously differ. It is my conviction that the church is first and foremost that community of people who gather to celebrate and bear witness to God's redemptive activity in the world. We are here to proclaim in word and behavior that God's love for the world—acted out in the life, death, and resurrection of Jesus Christ—makes a difference in the way human beings live with themselves and with one another. We are here to proclaim a particular view of human community; a view that we seek to model, however imperfectly, in those gatherings of Christians often referred to as the local congregation. We gather together in communities of faith to be empowered to penetrate the world around us. This is what we are about. This gathering and scattering is at the heart of the Christian ministry.

We are confronted today with value questions of tremendous consequence. In many instances they affect the very existence of the human race. For centuries we have made human progress synonymous with economic growth and increased consumption. But shortages of key resources and increasing pollution have caused us to call our very way of life into question. We have built a civilization on the assumption that it was our God-given right to conquer and exploit nature only to discover that our exploitation has brought us to the brink of disaster. We are haunted by the specters of racism, war, and poverty as we struggle to conceive of a vision of human destiny that will enhance the value of life and the possibility of human community. The answers to these questions will be worked out in the ongoing dialogue that takes place in every corner of the globe at every level of society—a dialogue that touches the very heart of the Gospel. And yet, as the Christian Church now stands, we are not equipped to participate in this dialogue; and we will not be until we build into its very structures a genuinely mutual ministry of the ordained and non-ordained.

When the New Testament speaks of the *laos,* the people of God, it refers to the whole church, clergy and laity alike. "For Christ is like a single body," writes St. Paul, "with its many limbs and organs which, many as they are, together make up one body." All Christians would affirm this, but in practice genuine mutuality is the exception, not the rule. To recover this is the most serious task we face. It will mean, however, rethinking the very nature of the church and the way we are organized to carry out our work. In 1958, in his classic book, *A Theology of the Laity,* Henrick Kraemer suggests a perspective from which this rethinking might take place. "Everything in the Church and in the world (from the point of view of the Gospel) revolves around the so-called 'ordinary member of the Church.' For in him must become somehow visible that the Lordship of Christ over the Church and over the world is not a fairy tale or a gratuitous assertion, but a reality which 'bites.' The apparatus of the Church has to be directed towards that end," Kraemer continues. "Not towards the maintenance of historical institutions and formulations, as if they are sacrosanct and invisible. The total activity of the Church in its worship, its preaching, its teaching, its pastoral care, should have the purpose of helping the 'ordinary membership of the Church' to become what they are in Christ."[1]

II

After a year and a half of visiting churches and meeting with groups of clergy and laity, I am convinced that the greatest single obstacle to the genuine renewal of the church is the lack of mutuality that exists between the clergy and the laity. You hear it expressed in many different ways. Clergy complain of a sense of isolation. "I feel as if much of the time I am engaged in a tug-of-war which never quite surfaces," states one pastor. "It's not that I want it to be this way; it just seems to happen." Or as an active layman from a large suburban congregation puts it: "I think very highly of the clergy of our parish. It's just that I never seem to know where they are coming from. At times it feels that we are operating on totally different wavelengths." Obviously, this is not the whole story. There are numerous examples of extremely effective working relationships between clergy and laity, but the opposite is true in enough cases to cause us to view it as a problem of genuine seriousness.

Last year in order to get more data to support my concern, I wrote some fifty persons in the church (both clergy and lay) and asked them what they thought were some of the things that prevented the development of genuine mutuality in the total ministry of the church. Some issues emerged again and again. These are the factors they cited as the major blocks to genuine mutuality:

•Tremendous cultural pressures tend to keep the institutional church on the periphery of society. After all, we say religion is a personal matter. These pressures create great separation between the world of the church and the world of the marketplace, affecting the mind-set of both clergy and laity.

•The responsibility which the clergy feel for building up the congregation tends to make the needs of the congregation (for leadership, financial support, program help) the dominant agenda when clergy and lay persons are in conversation.

•Clergy are perceived as having a well-ordered, well-articulated set of beliefs and knowledge which make it difficult for lay persons to share their often less clear beliefs and questions without feeling childlike and sometimes foolish.

•The often unconscious conspiracy between lay persons and clergy produces a bargain in which both parties agree to certain conditions in return for certain rewards—just like marriage. One person (the clergy person) is allowed to feel in charge at the expense of feeling a little set apart and insecure. The other person (the lay person) is allowed to feel cared for and secure at the expense of feeling slightly inferior and with less power.

If the churches are to respond creatively to these factors and develop a sense of genuine mutuality, we need to become much more clear about the functions of ministry clergy and laity need to perform. I believe that the time is particularly ripe for this. We have come through a period in the church marked by a great lack of clarity about many things, not the least of which was our understanding of the nature and function of ministry. There are signs, however, that we are ready to move on. Fundamental to such movement lie several key elements that must be built into the life of the Church:

•The realization that to be on a pilgrimage is of greater value than having all the answers. In this context clergy and laity are fellow pilgrims. When the clergy are free of the "answer man" role, they are more able to hear.

•A system of accountability where both the ordained and lay leadership of the congregation are given feedback on the quality of the work they do. In some places this is done in a weekend conference, in others by a congregational questionnaire. The point is that it is done in a regular, disciplined manner.

•Opportunities for the clergy to learn from the laity (where the laity set the agenda) at sufficient depth so as to be able to offer support in the exercise of their ministries outside the institutional church as well as opportunities for the laity to hear from the clergy in depth about their fears, needs, and concerns so as to offer support to their ministries.

•Carefully designed and seriously pursued programs of lay theological education which is aimed at enabling laity to reflect on and interpret their daily experiences in light of what it means to be *laos* in the world.

•Recognition by clergy and laity that most of the crucial issues of mission are those which confront laity in the context of their daily lives, and that laity have both the credibility and the opportunity to exercise their ministry in ways that clergy often do not have.

As many of us can probably attest, much of this is already taking place in a variety of ways. It needs to take place more, however, as the essential prelude to developing functional models of what ministry is about. When we are clear about our functions we are in a position to prepare ourselves to exercise these functions more effectively.

III

Ministry is a function exercised in response to the prompting of the Holy Spirit. As St. Paul notes in his first letter to the Corinthians, "In each of us the Spirit is manifested in a particular way, for some particular purpose." Some ministries are quite personal and unique, based on the particular gift of a particular individual. Other ministries are broader in scope, shared in common by the Christian community as they seek to bear witness to the Gospel. If the Christian Church is to participate in the dialogue over the world's future, we need to begin clarifying how our gifts are expressed in ministry in both functional and theological terms. We need to know what ministry looks like and how we know when we are doing it. The function that we vest primarily in the clergy as representing the total community is that of celebrant or sacramentalist. All other functions they share with the total church by virtue of our common calling as the people of God.

For purposes of being clear about what we need to learn to do, we can identify four functions that seem to be of critical importance:

1) *We are storytellers.* We are sent into the world as people with a story to tell. Henri Nouwen writes: "Many of us have lost our sensitivity for our own history and experience our life as a capricious series of events over which we have no control. When our attention is drawn away from ourselves and absorbed by what happens around us, we become strangers to ourselves, people without a story to tell or to follow up."[2] As Christians, the story we live out is the story that has its focus in the person of Jesus Christ. It is a story that began before the world was created and will end only when God chooses to draw all things unto himself. It is a story of Abraham and a journey into the unknown. It is a story of Moses and liberation, of Job and his struggle to make sense out of misfortune, of Paul and his hymn to the power of faith in the search of self-worth. It is a story of how God has touched our lives in a thousand subtle ways. Ministry begins when we *own* this story—when we hear it, internalize it, feel it, participate in it, and tell it. If we are serious about ministry, we must be able to articulate the story of our redemption in ways others may hear.

2) *We are value bearers.* We are sent into the world to bear witness to a particular view of what is of primary value. The values we hold emerge out of the Gospel and touch on every segment of human existence. They hold up such things as the sacredness of human life, the worth and dignity of people, the

importance of honesty, the need to understand the created
order as a sacred trust, the ultimacy of love, and the terrible
destructiveness of human sin. When a young tennis player
receives half a million dollars for winning a tennis match on
a Saturday afternoon while the City of New York is laying off
thousands of employees for lack of funds, something is wrong
with our value system. The United States has not lost its vision
due to lack of resources or lack of imagination. We have lost
our vision due to the greed that permeates every level of our
society—and greed is a problem of value. Christian ministry
involves a continuous clarification, in the light of the Gospel,
of the values we ourselves hold, and a commitment to bear
witness to these values at every point where decisions are
made—no matter how small or insignificant that point may be.
To exercise this ministry we need continuous reflection and
support as we wrestle with the often agonizing decisions that
are placed before us. Where such an atmosphere does not exist,
it is up to us to create it. Nothing could be more important for
the future of the Christian ministry in our world.

3) *We are community builders.* We are concerned with deepening human community because we are the people of Pentecost,
and Pentecost is about the Spirit taking separated human beings and overcoming their estrangement. "In Christ there is
neither Jew nor Greek, slave nor free, male nor female, for we
are all one in Christ Jesus." Christ has broken down the "wall
of partition between us." This is our heritage and to act on this
heritage is our ministry. It is a ministry of listening, of healing,
and of caring. The parish church is intended to be a mi-
crocosm of the community to which we point. It is the mutual
ministry of clergy and laity to help this to be. Our towns and
our cities reflect vast separation between individuals and families and races and groups—sometimes quite unconscious,
sometimes quite deliberate. We live in a world at war—psy-
chologically if not actually. We are called to be peacemakers

at every level in which we function, for this is the meaning of Christian ministry. It is a ministry that requires skills in group development, conflict management, interpersonal awareness, as well as a profound and growing openness to the Spirit. God is the reconciler of persons, but we are called as ambassadors of reconciliation—a ministry that involves not only a deep capacity to care, but a high degree of wisdom and skill as well.

4) *We are spiritual journeyers.* We are people on a self-conscious spiritual pilgrimage. It is a journey that involves a deepening self-awareness and self-discipline. It is a journey in faith entered into with a community of people who meet weekly for "the breaking of bread and prayers." The word "spiritual" means many things to many people—some of which are helpful, some not. I believe it is an important word for anyone who is serious about ministry, for it is a word that clearly refers to that interior quality of human existence that separates authenticity from shallowness. I am interested in rebaptizing the word "spiritual," giving it new associations and new meanings. We desperately need a spirituality that emerges out of genuine thirst rather than out of a sense of ought. We need a "hard-nosed" spirituality free of religious piety and sentimentality. For spiritual growth is a way of describing our quest for wholeness. It involves all of life, and therefore, in relating us to the movement of God in human life, it must also relate us more deeply to ourselves and to the world in which we live. At the heart of ministry is self-conscious participation in the spiritual journey of the people of God. We cannot give to others what we have not found for ourselves.

IV

The ministry of the church is always the ministry of the *laos*. It is the mutual ministry of clergy and laity alike, each supporting and challenging the other in the unique functions they are called upon to perform. Colin Williams has identified two very critical functions a congregation must carry out if the laity are to understand and fulfill their ministry in the total mission of the church in the world. First of all, he notes, the congregation must be able to discern the different gifts of the Holy Spirit given to its members, and secondly, to develop structures that function to train and develop these gifts. "Many laymen are aware of their calling in this way," he writes, "but they fail to find a church structure to give them the help they need in relating the Gospel to the problems of trade unions, factory laws, labor and management, or the problems of industrial or rural communities in a fast changing society."[3]

"The world needs the Church and its moral leadership," writes Jeffrey Hadden, "to push, pull, and shove us deep inside ourselves, and then out to the front line."[4] For the laity this ministry is primarily in society at large and secondarily in the community of faith. For the parish clergy the opposite is, of necessity, true. They are set aside to administer the sacraments —to celebrate God's presence among his people, to preach, to teach, and to enable others to exercise the ministry they have been given. To do this effectively, however, they too must have support. There must be within every congregation a lay apostolate who, through a common discipline and concern, share the responsibility for building up the community of faith. This, of course, is the other side of mutuality. It involves the kind of collegiality that allows the clergy person to say, "I hurt" or "I need help" in an environment free from the fear of misunderstanding or reprisal. To bring about this kind of collegiality is no easy task.

A very active layman said quite honestly, "I want my minister to be a spiritiual leader. I don't want to hear about his problems and his doubts." Most clergy have heard this said so often that they have learned to be cautious—more comfortable "telling" than "sharing." Mutuality does not require that everyone relate the same way in all circumstances. It does, however, require commitment to a process in which the gifts of both clergy and laity can be affirmed and developed in an atmosphere of common commitment and trust.

In the body of Christ there are different gifts and different functions. This, however, is as far as the separation goes. For we are *all* storytellers. We are *all* value bearers and community builders. And, above all, we participate in a common journey.

Churches all over the country (indeed all over the world) are at present engaged in exciting and innovative efforts to recapture that sense of ministry that the church was given at Pentecost. Back in the 1950s there was much creative thinking about ministry, and it seems to have found new soil in which to be tested—a soil formed by the moral and social struggles of the 60s and now infused with a rediscovery of our spiritual roots. But whatever is emerging, one thing is certain. It will not last unless there are structural and attitudinal changes in the church to sustain what is begun. The forces at work against mutuality and mission are buried deep within our common life. Much will depend on the energy and the discipline and the care that we are willing to put to the task. Nothing, I believe, is of more importance.

Sidney Skirven put it this way, in words that serve as a wise and hopeful summary to what I have sought to express:

Christian ministry will always occur through earthen vessels: human beings and institutions. To eliminate human frailties is, obviously, not possible. What can be done is more modest and more profitable. Pastors and congregations can begin to probe into the internal dynamics of their common life together in an effort to understand what it is they are about. In that self-understanding, more truth and honesty about what it means to be the people of God in the world will prevail. And that is likely to provide increased self-awareness about individuals and institutions. If Christian ministry can begin to happen within the parish, then it is likely to happen beyond the parish in new and effective ways in the world.[5]

CHAPTER III

A People With a Story

Heaven and earth will pass away;
my words will never pass away.

MARK 13:31

I

"Religion, some think, is believing in doctrines, belonging to an organization, saving one's soul through an attitude (trust in God) or works," writes Michael Novak. "But there are countless ways of living out the same doctrine, many different ways of belonging, an endless number of ways of misperceiving one's own soul. This is why it seems better to imagine religion as the telling of a story with one's life."[1] Everyone's life, therefore, is shaped by a story. It could be a story of alienation, separation, discovery, or growth. A lot depends, of course, on our particular life histories—but not all. Behind everyone's personal story, there is a greater story, a cosmic story, that takes the many incoherent elements of our personal story and shapes them into a coherent pattern. This is the religious domain of story—the mysterious interaction between personal story and that underlying story that gives meaning to human existence. For the Christian this underlying cosmic story is embodied in the biblical story of redemption, culminating in the life, death, and resurrection of Jesus Christ.

One way in which we "do" ministry is in telling the story of how human life is made new by the creative power of God.

33

Telling the story, however, implies more than the mere recitation of words—even sacred words. We "do" ministry when we speak or act in a way that reveals to others the mystery of that interaction between personal story and cosmic story. It involves telling the story in a way that reveals not only something of our own lives but, at a deeper level, a glimpse of that underlying reality in which we see, if only for a moment, the mystery of human existence. The ministry of storytelling is something quite different than telling a stranger that "Jesus saves." It is a ministry in which our own stories, spoken or unspoken, become the vehicle for the divine human encounter.

Recently we have begun to see a significant rediscovery of the crucial importance of folk tales, fables, fairy tales, sagas, legends, and myths to the life of faith. The work of Fr. John Dunne of Notre Dame, the Lutheran theologian, Robert Roth, and the ealier work of Sam Keen were my sources of initiation. But since that time I have been deeply enriched by the explorations of James William McLendon, Jr., Sally TeSelle, Michael Novak, and most recently, Urban Holmes;[2] as well as the deep probings into the cultural and psychological roots of story given to us by such giants as Joseph Campbell and Carl Jung. Underlying the work of all these persons is a very clear message. When we speak of "story," we are speaking of something deeply rooted in the mystery of human existence.

Although much in the Christian tradition has worked to keep this undertaking of story a vital part of our heritage, we have also contributed to its distortion in our efforts to moralize and ritualize religious experience. All too often, personal witness or religious testimony say more about our need for certainty than they do about the deeper dimensions of our encounter with the mystery of God. Storytelling is serious business. It takes us beyond simple illustration, or the narcissistic need to talk about ourselves, into those experiences of human life that have a certain universal quality about them. Storytelling is an act of ministry because by grace it is possible for us to become bearers of what is most sacred in human life.

Generally speaking, stories that serve as vehicles of the divine-human encounter reflect four fundamental characteristics. First of all, they have an open-ended quality about them that opens us up to the great questions of life in a way that encourages exploration and growth. Twelve years ago I shared with two friends my frustration over the way my job was going. I was encountering resistance and confusion that I couldn't quite put my finger on, and yet knew existed. After an hour or so of sharing my burdens with them, one of my friends said to me quite simply and directly, "Jim, did you ever stop to consider that the problem is *you?*" I shall never forget that moment as long as I live. It was as if I had been confronted at the deepest level of my existence. The emotions that were surging within me were so great that I couldn't respond—at least not then. I mark that moment, however, as the beginning of a long and painful struggle to find the meaning of my own personal journey. It was as if the God who spoke to Adam had said also to me: "Where are you?"

Secondly, storytelling, as we are describing it, reflects the drama of our struggle to comprehend the unknown. Whether it be the story of Jacob wrestling with an angel or my own struggle for faith, the same quality is present. As James B. Wiggins writes: "A story of real importance is not an argument so much as it is a presentation and an invitation. It presents a realm of experience accessible through the imagination and invites participation in imaginative responses to reality, indeed to respond to reality as imaginative."[3]

Thirdly, story deals consistently with the profound themes of human existence, themes of bondage and deliverance, separation and reunion, life and death. When a child is able to share with you the story of being lost in a crowded department store, enveloped in sheer terror, and suddenly to look up and see the outstretched arms of a loving parent, you are listening to a story of profound consequence. It is a story that has been told and retold in every setting in which men or women have found themselves.

Fourthly, serious storytelling has the potential for initiating us into the mystery of our own being. When a child asks, "Daddy, tell me about when you were a little boy," he is inquiring into his origins—into that time with which we are intimately connected, yet not present to observe.

The English word "religion" derives from the Latin word *ligare*, from which we get the word "ligament," meaning "to bind together." *Re-ligio* brings to mind all that acts in life to bind together a lost wholeness. The restoration of that unity which is a part of our past—that sense of rootedness from which identity springs—comes partly by the telling and retelling of particular stories. "What kind of story are we in?" asks John Dunne in his book *Time and Myth*. "Is it a story of an adventure, a journey, a voyage of discovery? Or is it something simpler like the child playing by the sea? If we are in the story of an adventure, a journey, a voyage of discovery, we are in a story where time is all important. Our journey may in fact be a quest of life like that of Gilgamesh, carrying us to the boundaries of life in an effort to conquer death. Or it may be a return from the boundaries, a journey like that of Odysseus, carrying us from the wonderland of death back into the life that can be lived within the boundaries set for us by time. The *awareness* that my own personal story—that story which I alone can tell —is intimately connected with those universal stories which give meaning to human existence is a prelude to faith. Christian faith emerges when deep within us we become aware that our own story and the Gospel story are one and the same."[4]

At the heart of all it means to be the *laos*—the people of God

—is the ministry of storytelling. Underlying this ministry is the hard work of owning our own story in the context of that larger story which is our heritage in Christ.

II

There are many definitions of the Christian Church, all of which seek to emphasize some particular element of what is obviously a many faceted phenomenon. One way of describing the Church is simply to affirm that we are a people with a story. Our sense of rootedness, our identity, our very world-view has been shaped and reshaped by a story that has been proclaimed in word and deed down through the centuries. We are a people of holy memory, formed by those great biblical images that give substance to our faith. For a moment let your memory bring into the present the figure of Abraham who ventured forth in faith into an unknown land. Or Moses, who led our spiritual forebears out of bondage into freedom. Or Amos and Hosea, Jeremiah and Isaiah, who called us to repentance, lest justice and mercy be blotted from the face of the earth. Or the man Jesus, crucified, dead, and buried, who rose again in victory that all life might be made new. As James McClendon points out, these images are not merely peripheral to faith, they are the "very substance of religion." "Our doctrine, then, must be," he writes, "that men of biblical faith are those who find in Scripture what is centrally there—great dominant images, such as those of Kingdom of God, and Israel, and sacrifice, and Son of Man—*and who apply them as the makers of Scripture applied them*—to themselves."[5]

In my own faith journey, I find that four such images have tended to dominate my perception of the meaning of life. Quite obviously, in other people's lives other images have played the central part. I offer my own experience only as a way of showing how in one person's life images which are central to the biblical story intersect and empower our personal stories as well.

For as long as I can remember, the image of God as Creator has touched and energized my life story. I experience in the world a flow of energy which gives rise to creativity in all of its various forms. "Behold! I am making all things new!" affirms the Scripture. We call this creative energy, this life force, the love of God. It touches everything in the universe, holding all the parts together like an egg holds together the flour in a loaf of bread. I have experienced this creative energy, often despite myself. It comes as insight, excitement, love, healing, creativity—and sometimes as a deep sense of identification with the vast, continuously unfolding and interrelated process of life in which I am a tiny but nevertheless significant part.

I carry within me an image of a covenant between God and humankind that reaches back into the origins of time. It is a covenant both of accountability and forgiveness, calling us to a life of faithfulness in relation to the holiness of God and the needs of the human family. We are indeed "our brother's keeper," and we will be held accountable for the way in which we live out this responsibility. The biblical image of the covenant is an image of human and divine solidarity, of relatedness and moral responsibility. It is in relation to this deep sense of belonging that my sense of identity comes—the sense that who I am and who I will become is tied up with my capacity to live with integrity and compassion in relation to the human family of which I am a part. It is a sense that who I am is intimately connected with my capacity for relationships of depth which, at the deepest level, I both yearn for and resist. When grasped by this image of the covenant, I am aware that the freedom and possibility I experience in life is somehow bound up in the figure of the man Jesus, who in some incredible life-giving way makes himself present in the deep places of my life. I have a sense—sometimes fleeting, sometimes very real—of what St. Paul meant when he said, "It is no longer I who live, but Christ who lives in me." It is this awareness that calls me into covenant with the mystery of life whom we call God.

At the heart of the biblical story is the image of life emerging out of death. For Christians this is the Easter story—that image of new life which moved that first apostolic community from mourning into celebration. In my own life, it is this image that probably is the root image of my faith. Until I am forced to die to my need to control the outcome of what I offer to another, I cannot love—and without love, I cannot live. "Anyone who wishes to be a follower of mine must leave self behind; he must take up his cross, and come with me. Whoever cares for his own safety is lost, but if a man will let himself be lost for my sake and for the Gospel, that man is safe. What does a man gain by winning the whole world at the cost of his true self?" (Mk 8:34–36)

It is this image that calls me—often painfully and haltingly —into the dark places of failure, fear, and guilt. I have experienced death in myself and in others. Death is an ever-present reality. But so also is life. I know what it means to feel energy and hope creeping back into the psyche when everything around seems dark and lifeless. It is the awareness that despite the ravages of greed and hate and disease, life does indeed break through in such a way that I am enabled to affirm in my own life that which the Gospel story holds to be true.

The fourth biblical image that has so profoundly shaped my understanding of the world is that proclaimed by Jesus in the earliest days of his ministry. He said simply: "The kingdom of God has come." This same statement is made in a number of ways throughout the New Testament. "The kingdom of God is upon you" or "among you" or "within you." All these reflect the same basic image—that of power breaking into human experience, releasing us from the bondage of those demonic forces that grip us both as individuals and as a society, and calling us—if only momentarily—into genuine human community. When I am grasped by the image of the kingdom of God, I know that genuine interdependence and community within the human family is possible. What we experience now is but a taste of what will be. It is through the image of the kingdom that I experience what it means to say that "Christ is Lord." The destructiveness of human sin—the greed and the injustice and the arrogance—that so plagues the human community is not the last word. Christ is risen and the kingdom of God is here. We are part of a story that knows this to be true.

The ministry of storytelling is at the heart of the Church's calling. Internally, it involves work with our own stories in relation to those great images that emerge from the Scriptures. Externally, it involves sharing our story with others so that the mystery of God acting in our lives might be the source of new possibility not only for the Church, but for the world in which we live.

III

Storytelling is both a ministry within the community of faith and a ministry to the world at large. When it takes place within the community of faith it is a ministry of renewal. When it takes place outside, it is a ministry of evangelism. It is the aim of this section to explore both of these aspects of storytelling in terms of their implications for ministry and for parish life.

Renewal takes place in a congregation when, through the work of the Holy Spirit, persons are opened to one another and to the power of the Gospel story to make a difference in the quality of their lives. The ministry of storytelling is a vehicle for this happening. When opportunities are created for people to wrestle with the meaning of story for themselves and for one another, a process is begun that has profound implications for personal faith and commitment. Three aspects of this ministry are of particular importance. First of all, serious storytelling provides an opportunity for people to stay in touch with that life process that is so vital to personal and spiritual growth. As Sidney Jouard wrote in *The Transparent Self*, "Self-disclosure is a symptom of personality health and a means of ultimately achieving healthy personality."[6] Most of us need help with this, and what better place to find help than in that institution committed to the enhancement of the abundant life of which Jesus speaks.

The second creative aspect of storytelling within the congregation is the simple fact that it contributes to genuine trust and openness. We learn to trust those persons with whom we can share our lives. A storytelling ministry is a way of sustaining that community given to us by the Spirit. It is a way of enhancing those forces that make for vitality and growth.

Finally, the ministry of storytelling aims at creating those settings where the encounter between the Gospel story and our own personal stories can take place. It is a ministry aimed at nourishment and depth. One church sought to strengthen this aspect of its ministry through a weekend training conference in which people were given the opportunity simply to practice telling stories. As the conference began, participants were given the following orientation:

Throughout history, one of man's most effective ways of communicating his sense of life's deepest meanings has been through telling stories. We are going to try sharing with each other some of our own perceptions of life's meaning through this medium. Saturday, we will divide into small groups and each person will be asked to take a turn (a) telling a story; (b) listening silently while the others react to it and discuss it; and then (c) joining the others in a wrap-up discussion.

By tomorrow morning, please think of a story you can tell in 10 minutes or less, which expresses some aspect of your personal "theology" (that is, your view of the world, God, or the meaning of life). Don't struggle to find something to express your deepest, most central belief. Whatever comes easily to mind and expresses something meaningful to you will do. Don't panic.[7]

Other instructions included permission to use any kind of story—historical, biblical, fictional, personal—anything. People were asked simply to begin, "This is a story of . . ." And then, "Once upon a time . . ." The conference was highly successful but—like all interventions into the life of a congregation—made sense only to the degree that it was part of an ongoing process.

The ministry of storytelling *outside* the community of faith is a ministry of evangelism. Although sometimes misused in the church, evangelism is a profoundly biblical word. In the New Testament, an evangelist is one who proclaims the "evangel," the good news or Gospel of Christ. The aim of the evangelistic task is always conversion, that is, to present the good news in such a way that I am drawn into the mystery of the One who not only stands within my story but gives meaning to it. Conversion is a gift of grace that frees me from bondage to myself and calls me into relationship with Jesus Christ. It reveals my story to me in a different dimension. As William Stringfellow wrote some years ago, "Evangelism is not essentially verbal, even though it seems commonly to be believed that the recitation of certain words constitutes efficacious evangelism. Evangelism consists of loving another human being in a way which represents for him the care of God for his particular life. Evangelism rests upon the appeal to another man to remember his own creation—to remember

Who made him and for Whom he was made. Evangelism is the event in which a Christian confronts another man in a way which assures the other man that the new life which he observes in the Christian is vouchsafed for him also."[8]

One of the problems a storytelling ministry always confronts is that of wordiness and spiritual imperialism. When either occurs, the evangelistic message is blocked because we have been cut off from our own stories. Words are an easy substitute for authenticity. Spiritual imperialism—"laying on" answers or formulae without regard to the integrity of the persons to whom we are speaking—is a substitute for having to face the deep places in our own lives. It is easier to "tell" than to "be." I am convinced that one of the attractions of many Westerners to Eastern mysticism is its essential wordlessness. In the West we are inundated with words. For many, the Church is part and parcel of this inundation. We appear to talk more than we feel, using words before we have engaged in the hard task of internalizing their meaning in our own lives.

The ministry of storytelling, then, is essentially dialogical— a means of connecting with another human being in ways that take us beneath the surface. Its aim is conversion, not in the sense of bringing others around to our point of view but in inviting them in the name of Christ to enter into their own stories in order that they might find meaning and fulfillment for themselves. In an interview with Jean Woolfolk at the Nairobi Assembly of the World Council of Churches, the issue was stated with profound clarity:

I believe that the living Christ is the agent of conversion. To speak in parables or images: Christ is not *with* me, the evangelist. He is *between* me, "the witness," and him, "the listener." I point to Christ. I draw a picture of him. I tell his story. But hopefully it is Christ himself who finally meets the other person. This meeting, a sacred one, is conditioned by my services, but it is also transcendent. Because He is present, He lives. And this is the reason why the miracle happens—the miracle in which we, the talker and the listener, are *both* converts. I must look again at Christ, because my brother points to him."[9]

Storytelling is sacred business. For it to remain authentic, it must continuously raise up the great questions in human existence for which there are no answers. When I share my story with someone else, I point both to Christ and to that mystery who stands beyond all that we know and can yet experience. It is here that we stand on common ground with all humankind, converted or unconverted, Christian, Buddhist, or Jew.

The ministry of storytelling is a critical function of the Christian community. We have a story to tell, and for the sake of the world we need to tell it, not in arrogance but in openness to him who calls us to an ever-deepening experience of our own stories—stories that in Christ have cosmic significance. "The guru instructs by metaphor and parable," writes Sheldon Kopp, "but the pilgrim learns through the telling of his own tale. Each man's identity is an emergent of the myths, rituals, and corporate legends of his culture, compounded with the epic of his own personal history. In either case, it is the compelling power of the storytelling that distinguishes men from beasts. The paradoxical interstice of power and vulnerability which makes a man most human rests on his knowing who he is right now, because he can remember who he has been, and because he knows what he hopes to become. All this comes of the wonder of his being able to tell his tale."[10]

"In Christ indeed we have been given our share in the heritage [story], as was decreed in his design whose purpose is everywhere at work" (Eph 1:11).

CHAPTER IV

Values and a Changing Society

These are the words of the Amen, the faithful
and true witness, the prime source of all God's
creation: I know all your ways; you are neither
hot nor cold. How I wish you were either hot
or cold! But because you are lukewarm, neither
hot nor cold, I will spit you out of my mouth.
REVELATIONS 3:15–16

I

In times of transition vacuums emerge in which new values are born. This birthing process is neither easy nor quick. It requires a procedure of sorting and sifting those elements that come to us from many levels of our experience until a new construct is born that can and does empower action. After a decade of social and political upheaval, we continue to be in such a transition. Old values are dying and new values are being born in a process which is of critical importance to the Christian Church. If those values proclaimed in the Gospel are to have any place in the world that is emerging, Christians who are clear about what these values are must be part of this process.

Herein lies the heart of the challenge. As Jeffrey Hadden points out, "Those who sit in the pews are essentially no different in their attitudes toward principles of social justice, conceptions of brotherhood, laws and the like from those who never set foot in the church. Until evidence indicates that those inside the churches are more vitally committed to the Christian ideals of the Gospels than is the man on the street, there is little to be excited about."[1] It is quite possible, however, for the very challenge presented by this statement to be itself a source of excitement. It is fundamental to the very nature of the local church to confront this challenge. To do so, we must raise up and support a ministry of value bearers who are willing and able to enter into those dialogues and debates from which vacuums are filled.

Values are more than the ideals or moral absolutes to which we aspire. A value is an inner construct blending together religious beliefs, ethical principles, societal norms, and life experiences in a way that empowers us to act. Everything we do, be it the decisions we make or the actions we take during the course of a day, is based on some consciously or unconsciously held value. Values are freely held and important enough to cause us to want to act on their behalf. One of the things that makes me unique is the particular value structure that empowers my life. There are elements of this structure that I might hold in common with others, but the particular combination is mine. This means, of course, that Christians can agree on certain ethical principles and yet live their lives differently. It is our values that create and sustain our lifestyle.

Charles Gore, the late Anglican Bishop of Oxford, is reported to have said that "man's first duty is not to follow his conscience, but to enlighten it." If we are to be value bearers in society in the name of Christ, then it is of critical importance that the values we hold be somehow shaped by encounter with the person of Jesus. Such encounter will obviously take seriously his teaching, but at a deeper level it will seek to experience through the Gospel narratives the values that seemed to shape his life and ministry. Obviously, such an experience is highly subjective and needs to be balanced against the ongoing tradition of the Christian community as well as the day-to-day perceptions of those Christians who share our journey. Nevertheless, there is no avoiding this encounter with the Gospels if we are to take the business of value bearing seriously.

In my own encounter with the Jesus of the Gospels, four value constructs emerge for me as particularly significant both in terms of their consistency in his life and their impact on my own. In identifying these I am simply saying that at the present time these are the values that confront me as I try to live a style of life that is consistent with my experience of the Gospel. The ways these are expressed quite obviously reflect some of the other elements that impinge upon my life and help to make up my own particular value system. They are offered as a way of entering into dialogue with the values of others.

First of all, undergirding the life and ministry of Jesus was a commitment to maintain a close personal relationship with the Father. Jesus' life was shaped by the will of God as this was perceived and understood in those deep and continuous moments of communion that were one of the marks of his life. "He went away to a lonely spot and remained there in prayer" (Mk 1:35). "He sent the people away; ... he went up the hill-side to pray alone" (Mt 14:23). "My Father," he prayed during those dark moments at Gethsemane, "if it is not possible for this cup to pass me by without my drinking it, thy will be done" (Mt 26:42). Solitude, communion, a sense of interconnectedness with the Father—these were not simply principles in Jesus' life, these were values by which he lived. His life was an affirmation that human existence is most real when it is consistently nourished from within.

Secondly, Jesus gave greater value to people and their needs than to the institutional structures that ordered their life. "The Sabbath was made for the sake of man and not man for the Sabbath (Mk 2:27)," he said after plucking corn contrary to proscribed tradition. Jesus unmasked the pretensions of the principalities and powers—the institutions, the ideologies, the images, the beliefs, indeed, the very ethos through which civilization is shaped and transmitted—by his refusal to submit to their claim of ultimate authority. We need governments and customs and social structures to order our existence, but like all of creation, when any institution or ideology is cut off from the purposes of God and claims sovereignty for itself, that which was created good becomes demonic. Anyone who has ever viewed an angry mob or a government obsessed with its own omnipotence knows how frightening this power can be. It is as if the "mob" or the "government" takes on a personality of its own which, in turn, becomes the personality of the individual members. John Yoder writes in *The Politics of Jesus:* "Man's subordination to these Powers is what makes him human, for if they did not exist there would be no history nor society nor humanity. If then God is going to save man *in his humanity*, the Powers cannot simply be destroyed or set aside or ignored. Their sovereignty must be broken. This is what Jesus did, concretely and historically, by living among man a genuinely free and human existence. . . . Here we have for the first time . . . a man who is not a slave of any power, of any law or custom, community or institution, value or theory. . . . Not even to save his own life. . . ."[2] This freedom to unmask the pretensions of those structures that claim ultimate authority at the expense of human need and human worth was a key value which shaped the life and ministry of Jesus. It is a value that each of us must encounter at some point.

A third key value can be clearly seen in the way Jesus sought to serve life rather than control it. This was the secret of human fulfillment because it was the purpose for which we were created. "For even the Son of Man did not come to be served but to serve, and to surrender his life as a ransom for many" (Mk 10:45). This is what he said and this is how he lived.

His life was one of love in action lived with passionate intensity. He knew what his life was for and he lived it to the fullest. To embrace, as a value, reaching out to others without personal reward for oneself implies also embracing a series of related values. It involves believing that loving is more important than winning, that being able to be vulnerable is more important than possessing power, that setting someone free to find the best in themselves is better than managing other people's lives, that being able to risk not knowing is more important than being certain about all things. Jesus said: "By gaining his life a man will lose it; by losing his life for my sake, he will gain it" (Mt 10:39). It is a strange value indeed—paradoxical and mysterious—leading not to fame but to a cross. And yet as life attests, it is the only value that makes community possible; a value without which the world would be tragically bereft.

Lastly, Jesus lived his life in identification with the poor and the oppressed. He valued the empowerment of those whom society had left without power. "The spirit of the Lord is upon me," he publicly proclaimed. "He has sent me to announce good news to the poor" (Lk 4:18). In the established churches of the West we have so domesticated and romanticized this value that it has ceased to be a value any longer. It has become at best a principle without bite, to our own tragic detriment. Jesus stood alongside the lepers and the paralytics, the poor and the outcast, the prostitutes and the tax collectors. He was offensive to those who were religiously upright and a threat to those who had political power. He lived this way, not to be offensive for the sake of offensiveness, but to open our eyes to see what our comfort prevents us from seeing.

To become a disciple means to see for oneself the values that energized the life of Jesus of Nazareth, to struggle with them, until there comes that moment when by the grace of God they become our own. Commitment to an ongoing and disciplined enrichment of our relationship to God, the affirmation of human need and worth in the face of the demonic pretensions of those principalities and powers that control our lives, the desire to serve life out of love rather than power or reward, and a deep identification with the poor and the hungry and the oppressed; these are values that we can see in the life of Jesus. They are values which when affirmed and lived will make a profound difference in the quality of life of the world that is emerging. It is through psychic and spiritual intercourse with values such as these that we are called to be value bearers in the name of Christ.

II

New values are born in the context of relationships that both challenge and support. It is the task of the local church to provide these kinds of relationships. It is in the community of the church that I can expect to have old values confronted and opportunity given for new values to be conceived, born, and tested. The problem arises when the church itself becomes a buttress against this very process of value clarification which is so essential to its life and ministry. If we are to raise up and sustain a value bearing ministry, we need churches that are themselves open to change—not on the basis of what's new is therefore good but on some clearly thought out criteria as to which changes are life-giving and which are destructive. In this section I would like to address this question of criteria before looking at how the local church goes about training and supporting a value bearing ministry.

If there is one word that buffeted the ears of most of us during the past fifteen years, it is the word "change." "Change" is the reason we give for everything. We defend doing what we plan to do anyway by referring to the inevitability of change. We excuse irresponsible behavior by pointing out how values are changing. Or else, taking an opposite tact, we view change as leading always to the destruction of those things we hold dear. It is as if all change is exactly the same and, by its very nature, God-ordained. The plain truth is that all change is not the same, nor is it inevitable. Change is ambiguous. At one level it is taking place all the time; at another, it is quite deliberate and planned. It can be creative or destructive, depending, of course, on the forces which are at work and the values which are inherent in the process. We are passive victims only to the degree that we cease to interact consciously with what happens to us. We are helpless only when our values and convictions cease to be part of the process.

Probably at no other time, however, has this issue of change been any more perplexing, or our feelings of helplessness any more acute, than they are today. In his best-selling commentary on change, *Future Shock*, Alvin Toffler attributes this to what he calls the "bursting of boundaries." "We have not merely extended the scope and scale of change," he writes, "we have radically altered its pace. We have in our time released a totally new social force—a stream of change so accelerated that it influences our sense of time, revolutionizes the tempo of daily life, and affects the very way we 'feel' the world around us. And this is the ultimate difference." Toffler continues, "We no longer 'feel' as men did in the past. This is the distinction that separates the truly contemporary man from all others. For this acceleration lies behind the impermanence—the transience—that penetrates and tinctures our consciousness, radically affecting the way we relate to other people, to things, to the entire universe of ideas, art and values."[3]

It is in the context of this kind of world that the church must address its mission. In doing this, however, we have a dual function. We are called upon to preserve that heritage from the past out of which countless millions have discovered both the meaning and purpose of their lives, while at the same time creating an environment that will enable these same persons —and this includes all of us—to move out into the unknown with courage and hope. From this perspective, not all change is good, nor is it inevitable. What we make of what we see depends on the place where we ourselves stand.

The criteria we bring to the evaluation of change emerge out of two models developed in the nineteenth century. These are generally referred to as order and conflict models of society. The order model is based on the assumption that harmony and balance are normative for human existence. Social problems emerge when the system which orders human existence becomes out of balance and dysfunctional. They are the result of weakened social control, inadequate institutionalization of goals, along with inadequate means for achieving these goals. Our response, therefore, to social dysfunction involves clarification of goals and procedures, while working toward some measure of consensus. The goal is to maximize that sense of harmony and balance which gives order to human existence.

The conflict model of society views the same data from a quite different perspective. Conflict theorists are alike in their rejection of the order model of contemporary society. They interpret order analysis as the strategy of a ruling group—a rationalization for more effective social control. The continually contested struggle between groups with opposing goals and worldviews is not an interruption to what is normative, but is itself normative. Harmony and balance are the interruptions. Social problems, therefore, reflect, not the administrative problems of a social system, nor the failure of individuals to perform their roles effectively, but rather, the adaptive failure of society to meet changing individual and group needs.

If we view a particular issue from a conflict model of social change, we will see things very differently from someone, equally well intentioned, who views the same facts from an order model of social change. During the 1960s many persons committed to the overall objective of the Civil Rights Movement strongly objected to methods which involved confrontation and social disruption. Others, however, viewed confrontation and disruption as the outpouring of energy necessary for a vital society. Genuine dialogue between those operating from these two quite distinct models of what is normative is as difficult as mixing apples and oranges and calling them by the same name.

We all view change from some particular point of view—often unidentified. But, unfortunately, at the level of the day-to-day decisions we need to make we are not very consistent. For most of us, the order model of change is the primary model simply because when life feels ordered and at peace we feel most secure. We begin to operate from a conflict model when we feel cut off from sources of power and are disillusioned about the possibility of our values and convictions ever becoming normative. Often the shift from an order to a conflict model is not even conscious; we simply begin to see things a different way. The development of any criteria for the evaluation of change, therefore, must begin with a fundamental assessment of what we believe to be normative. When we are clear about this, in the variety of situations which confront us, it is possible to build other criteria that will enable us to interact with our environment with some consistency and strength.

The order and conflict perspectives are two polar ways of looking at change, each with its own values and assumptions. The Christian faith is neither always affirming of order nor is it always affirming of conflict. St. Augustine, because of what he saw happening in the city of Rome, tended to view change through a conflict perspective. St. Thomas Aquinas, however, with his hierarchical view of the nature of things, viewed change from an order perspective. The point is, every situation presents its own particular set of issues. Other criteria, therefore, must be brought to bear by which we look at either the moral quality of stability on the one hand, or change on the other.

There are five criteria by which we Christians might evaluate each change that confronts us:

1. Does it facilitate justice?
2. Does it affirm the value and dignity of human life?
3. Does it produce a positive systemic impact?
4. Does it provide a fresh connectedness with what has gone on before?
5. Does it keep the door open to the future?

Priorities are affected by what is most urgent. In some situations, justice must take priority. In others, it is more urgent that the door be kept open to the future. Our decisions are made knowing full well that in most situations "we see through a glass darkly." Let us look then at the criteria.

First of all, does it facilitate justice? Justice is defined here as that which produces the greatest good for those who are the farthest from the centers of power. Jesus said: "I tell you this: anything you have done to one of my brothers here, however humble, you did for me" (Mt 25:40). From the Christian perspective change is good when it facilitates justice. It is less than good, to the point of being demonic, when it does not.

Secondly, the Gospel is unswerving in its commitment to the value and dignity of human life. "Even the hairs of your head have all been counted" (Mt 10:30). No change can be affirmed as consistent with the Christian tradition that would devalue the sanctity of human life, even to achieve the most noble ends. "All who take the sword die by the sword" (Mt 26:52). This lesson, which we seem consistently to have rejected, has come back to haunt us time and time again. We affirm that in the death and resurrection of Jesus of Nazareth, the life of every human being in all times and in all places is forever given infinite worth.

Thirdly, no change occurs in isolation. All life is systemic. Any change occurring in one part of the system will have a profound effect on every other part of the system as well. As Paul writes, "If one organ suffers, they all suffer together. If one flourishes, they all rejoice together" (1 Cor 12:26). It is equally true that change is not without cost. A positive impact on some part of the system will inevitably produce a negative impact in other parts. In evaluating change, therefore, we must ask: "Does the positive impact outweigh those ramifications which seem to be negative? Is the promise significant enough to outweigh the cost?"

Fourthly, does the change provide a fresh connectedness with what has gone on before? We are a people who emerge out of a very special story. Our task is to act in every generation in ways that enable people to share in the story we proclaim to be the source of life. Jesus repeatedly challenged the tradition from which he had come, but he never broke from it. He was a fulfiller, not a destroyer. All change emerges out of something which precedes it. We must simply ask: "Does what we see build on those sources of creativity and life which we have inherited, or does it cut us off from them?"

And, finally: Does what we perceive to be happening keep the doors open to the future, or does it shut off our options? Much of the change that occurs in human experience confronts us with new possibilities, without which we would atrophy and die. It is the Christian affirmation that this kind of change is the result of the ongoing creativity of God. Creation continues. But it is also true that some change is retrogressive. It would move us into blind alleys and close off our options for vitality and new life. Simply stated, it behooves us to know the difference as best we can determine.

These are five criteria by which we might evaluate the changes that confront us. For purposes of illustration, let me put some of them to the test. As a delegate to the General Convention of the Episcopal Church in 1967, I believed very firmly in the action of that Convention establishing the General Convention Special Program (GCSP). This action directed the Episcopal Church to set aside a major part of the national budget for the empowerment of the poor and politically dispossessed. It was the first criterion that shaped my decision. It seemed to me to be the *just* thing to do.

The second criterion also seemed to apply. Our action did indeed affirm the value and dignity of human life. Others felt quite strongly that the action we had taken also involved what I have suggested to be a fourth criterion, a fresh connection with the Gospel tradition. We saw this as a way of presenting the Gospel in a new way.

At the 1973 General Convention, this program was, for all intents and purposes, rejected by the Episcopal Church. Why? Applying the third criterion, the majority of persons present felt that the negative impact on the total system of the church —namely the individual dioceses—far outweighed whatever positive good had been accomplished. Others were disillusioned because the fourth criterion had not held up. The GCSP had not been seen by those who benefited from it as a fresh connection with the Gospel story. It was an experience of change from which the church learned much and, I believe, fulfilled the last criterion by keeping open, at a very critical time, the door to continued involvement in one of the world's most serious problems. Whether this is true or not, only time will tell, since the problem GCSP sought to address has not gone away. The point is that without criteria there is no way to evaluate the changes which impact us.

What then are we to make of the changes facing us in the

church today, changes which in most part reflect even far greater changes in the world around us? Obviously, all of us have to make that determination for ourselves. We have to be clear about where we stand so that our commitment is undiluted, while at the same time we must find ways of affirming the diversity which is part and parcel of our common life.

Robert Pirsig, in *Zen and the Art of Motorcycle Maintenance*, makes a comment which strikes me as particularly helpful. "We are living in topsy-turvy times," he writes, "and I think that which causes the topsy-turvy feeling is inadequacy of old forms of thought to deal with new experiences." "I've heard it said," Persig continues, "that the only real learning results from hang-ups, where instead of expanding the branches of what you already know, you have to stop and drift laterally for a while until you come across something which allows you to expand the roots of what you already know. Everyone's familiar with that. I think the same thing occurs with whole civilizations when expansion's needed at the roots."[4]

Expansion at the roots suggests to me a time when we work seriously at the task of examining our values. We have been so busy keeping up with ourselves that we have neglected to wrestle with such fundamental questions as: "Why are we doing what we are doing?" "Are the expected results worth the side effects?" "Just because we have always done it this way, does it mean there are no other possibilities worth considering?" Roots are expanded when we are able to view old situations with a new vision. It involves not only a fundamental change in how we think but also how we feel. We are passive victims of change only to the degree that we cease to respond consciously to the things that happen to us. We are helpless only when our values and convictions cease to be part of the process.

III

Economic scarcity, the increasing shortage of natural resources, the ever-widening gap between rich and poor are
forcing us to radically rethink, not only our values but our
very life-styles. What is being asked of us is a fundamental
redefinition of what is indeed essential. To be a value bearer
in the name of Christ is a critical function of ministry. The
local church, in cooperation with those agencies and institutions which are also addressing the question of values for a
changing world, has the task of equipping and supporting
these ministries to operate both within the church itself and
in the world at large.

A value-bearing ministry begins when a man or woman is
convinced of the need. This is where God's Word normally
first addresses us. This address could come through the medium of the Sunday sermon (a crucial vehicle for dealing with
the question of values in the context of the Gospel), through
a seminar, through a chance encounter, or through casual
conversation. When the address comes, there needs to be some
group or ongoing forum in the life of the congregation to
which the person can turn. It could be something as obvious
as a value-bearing ministry group or a Sunday forum on values
and life-styles. Adopting new values involves saying no to one
thing and yes to something new. It involves the painful process of "unpacking" old values of their emotional baggage,
particularly in those areas that most affect our economic security, political beliefs, or normal everyday life-style. It is very
difficult, for instance, for Americans to examine the question
of whether or not our present political or economic system is
indeed what is most needed for the years ahead. Immediately
specters of Communism or unbridled tyranny leap into our
consciousness. Nevertheless, underlying these questions are

values that need to be closely examined in the light of the Gospel.

The Gospel has much to say about the nature of change. The life, death, and resurrection of Jesus Christ brought revolutionary changes to the world, changes which by the power of the Spirit continue to make themselves felt. In the face of uncertainty, therefore, we stand not as those primed to defend at all costs what we have known, but as a people open to the promise of what lies ahead in Christ.

Many years ago Dietrich Bonhoeffer sounded a challenge to those who would respond to the value-bearing ministry to which we are called in baptism. His words have yet to be surpassed.

To do and dare—not what you would, but what is right. Never to hesitate over what is within your power, but boldly to grasp what lies before you. Not in the flight of fancy, but only in the deed there is freedom. Away with timidity and reluctance! Out into the story of events, sustained only by the commandment of God and your faith, and freedom will receive your spirit with exultation![5]

CHAPTER V

Building and
Sustaining Community

*What I mean is, that God was in Christ
reconciling the world to himself, no
longer holding men's misdeeds against
them, and that he has entrusted us with
the message of reconciliation. We come
therefore as Christ's ambassadors.*

2 CORINTHIANS 5:19

I

To participate in the building and sustaining of human community is to "do" ministry. It is the way in which we share
in the reconciling ministry of Christ. In the first section of this
chapter I would like to spell out briefly what in theological
terms we mean when we talk about "community," including,
from an experiential viewpoint, how Christ acts in the world
to bring it about. In the second and third sections I intend to
focus on what actually is involved in a community-building
ministry, both in the world-at-large and within the local
church. The last section will seek simply to ground our struggle for community within the context of worship, which, in
a very profound sense, is both an acting out and a celebration
of what community is all about.

In his letter to the Colossians, Paul writes: "In him [Christ]
everything in heaven and on earth was created, not only things
visible but also the invisible orders of thrones, sovereignties,
authorities, and powers: the whole universe has been created

through him and for him. And he exists before everything, and all things are held together in him. . . . Through him God chose to reconcile the whole universe to himself, making peace through the shedding of his blood upon the cross—to reconcile all things, whether on earth or in heaven, through him alone" (Col 1:15–17, 20). The image here is one of profound harmony and systemic interconnectedness emerging out of a sense of meaning and obedience. When this interconnectedness is experienced in the human sphere, we have what we call "community." The biblical word that most fully expresses this theological understanding of community is *shalom*, sometimes translated from the Hebrew as "peace." Shalom is an all-encompassing word covering all the many relationships of life and expressing a vision of what the Israelites conceived of as the ideal of what life was intended by God to be. In describing shalom, commentators use such words as "wholeness," "totality," "well-being," "the absence of violence or misfortune," "the untrammeled, free growth of the soul in conjunction with others," or "harmonious community." Or as a report of the World Council of Churches puts it: "Shalom is a social happening, an event in interpersonal relations." The report continues, "The goal towards which God is working, i.e., the ultimate end of his mission, is the establishment of the shalom, and this involves the realization of the full potentialities of all creation, and the ultimate reconciliation and unity in Christ. . . . Each time a man is imprisoned, tortured or destroyed, death is at work. But each time a man is a true neighbor, each time men live for others, the life giving action of God is to be discerned. These are signs of the Kingdom of God and of the setting up of shalom."[1]

The Church exists in the world as a sign of the kingdom. When we gather, we do so as an expression of shalom. In describing what this experience of Christian community is like, the New Testament uses the word, koinonia, or quite literally, "sharing in partnership" or "fellowship." As the author of the First Epistle of John writes, "If we walk in the light . . . we share together a common life [koinonia]" (1 Jn 1:7). God wills community. He intervenes in human history to heal the brokenness and disruption we have created. "To say Christ," writes Markus Barth, "means to say community, coexistence, a new life, peace."[2] It is from this understanding of God's intention for human existence that a ministry of community building emerges. We are not engaged in simply making life more pleasant. We are participating in what is fundamental to the redemptive activity of God.

The primary concern of the church is never with its own life alone, but with God's redemptive activity in the world. This activity is concerned with the reconciliation of the human family as we exist in relationship to each other and to the created order which sustains us. This redemptive activity of God—focused sharply in the person of Jesus Christ—involves the overcoming of the separation that exists between individuals, between groups, and between those structures in society that put nation against nation, race against race, man against woman, father against son, mother against daughter.

At the heart of the biblical message is a clear recognition of the reality of sin, that fundamental state of separation which touches all aspects of our existence. Sin describes the pressure that we experience within us to act on desires that we know are contrary to what we believe and what we want to be. It describes that innate lust for power that makes it so critical for us to be in control of the relationships and situations that involve us. Sin is rebellion against God's claim upon us—the urge to carve out our destinies in response only to our own limited and often distorted perceptions of reality. To understand the reality of sin in human existence is to understand why it is that all utopias are doomed ultimately to failure, why it is that power corrupts, why no institution or leader or

ideology can ultimately save us. To understand the awesome
reality of sin (attested to by the story of humankind in every
age and in every place) is to know the power of separateness
that exists within everyone—balanced only by the movement
of God pushing us out into communion with others who share
our humanity. There is available to everyone access to that
power which breaks through loneliness and isolation and calls
us into relationship with others. "When anyone is united to
Christ, there is a new world; the old order has gone, and a new
order has already begun (2 Cor. 5:17). The creation of this new
order, the re-creation of a world at one with itself (and therefore at one with God), is the redemptive activity of God in
Christ, that activity which men and women are called to celebrate, bear witness to, and, most importantly, participate in.
This is the fundamental task of the Christian Church.

One way of seeing God's redemptive activity in experiential
terms is to imagine that everyone exists in the world enclosed
in an invisible box. The inside walls of the box have a mirror
effect so that we perceive nothing that is not reflected in our
own image. I look at you, but what I see of you is influenced
by the way I perceive you responding to me. I relate to you,
and you relate to me separated from each other by the boxes
that, while seeming to protect, actually keep us in isolation.
The box, therefore, is another description of the problem of
sin. As a result, human relationships look something like this:

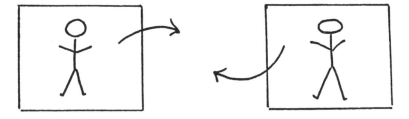

The Bible proclaims that God is continually present in the world countering the forces that keep us in isolation. He is continually calling us out of our boxes. In response to this pressure we peek out of our boxes in search for relationship. When we make contact with another person who is at the same time also moving out of his or her box, we experience that quality of relationship which gives meaning to human existence. It is this kind of encounter that gives birth to love. To meet another person outside of our boxes is to experience genuine community, a sign of the kingdom of God. The problem, of course, is that it occurs only for a brief moment, as if we were attached within our boxes by incredibly strong rubber bands. We stick our head out of our boxes, and almost immediately, we are jerked back in again until eventually, the rubber band begins to become more brittle and hard, and moving outside our boxes becomes less and less of a possibility.

Some years ago, while living in South Carolina, my wife and I were driving to the coast to spend several days with some friends. We had left our three small children with an excellent baby-sitter, which meant we were free to enjoy one another in a way that was different from our normal routine. As we drove away from home and the excitement had begun to subside, I was very much aware of a slight feeling of discomfort welling up within me, a sense that I needed to say something special, yet not knowing what. My wife told me later she had felt the same way. As a result, we said nothing, each waiting for the other to take the lead, each feeling a little let down, even lonely. We were very much within our boxes.

After an hour or so something quite powerful happened. It began with a word here, a gesture there, and suddenly there was a sense of deep connectedness. We didn't say much, we didn't need to. We were being drawn toward each other in a way that was almost beyond words, although words of honesty had paved the way. This experience of intimacy lasted about an hour and then passed. We had been drawn out of our boxes into communion and then returned to them again. Immediately after returning home, we tried to recreate that experience. To our surprise, we were suddenly involved in heated conflict, feeling cut off and separated. Before long it dawned on us what was happening. We were trying to create from within our boxes what God had done by calling us out. Genuine relationship is a gift. It cannot be manufactured or manipulated, only responded to and acted on.

One way of grasping the experiential nature of redemption is to see the action of Christ in the world freeing us from the ultimate imprisonment of our boxes. To describe Jesus as "sinless" is to see him as one who lived his life outside the box. He was indeed the "Man for others" because no human force could send him into isolation. His availability and openness to whomever and whatever came was constant, even unto death —and, more profoundly still, beyond death. As Paul wrote, "There is nothing in all creation that can separate us from the love of God in Christ Jesus our Lord" (Rom 8:39). The cross is the sign of his incredible freedom. On it he experienced the ultimate isolation anyone can know, yet his availability to the world never was broken. "Father, forgive them" is the greatest affirmation of freedom ever uttered. Easter affirms this cry. It is God's proclamation that not even the terrible and seemingly final isolation of death can force the Lord Christ into a box. He remains the sinless one, the open one, the whole man whose perception of reality is not through the mirror of self-protection but through the eyes of God.

On the interpersonal level the redemptive process might look something like this:

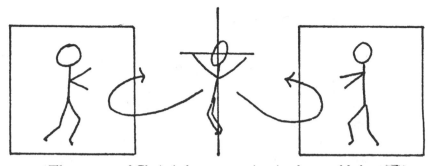

The power of Christ's love operating in the world through people and events calls us out of our boxes into relationship with him who will never withdraw. No matter what we do, the person of Jesus remains constant. It is through him, therefore, that our relatedness to others can be sustained. No one lives totally outside of his box, but nevertheless, the experience of freedom offered us by the Spirit is a reality that can be sustained under pressures that normally wouldn't seem possible. This is the redemptive promise, the promise of the Gospel of Christ.

The redemptive process, however, does not stop here. It is more than interpersonal; it involves every structure which separates the family of humankind. The bondage of sin not only holds us in individual boxes but in corporate boxes as well. In terms of our diagram, we look something like this:

The power of these structures is broken when we respond to the experience of freedom and the thirst for relatedness offered to us in the person of Christ. Whether or not the response is made consciously in the name of Jesus is of secondary importance. He is in the world calling men and women to himself whether we acknowledge him or not. Through those who appropriate his love, the structures of dehumanization and bondage are broken.

The ministry of Christ involves participation in the redemptive process. It involves the celebration of Christ's presence in the world. He is our hope, for nothing can ultimately separate him from relatedness to the human family. It involves moving out of our boxes, as the Spirit gives us strength, as agents of reconciliation in the world. It involves working to break down the walls of separation that exist between men and women, between groups and between nations so that we might indeed become what we were created to be. To function in this way in the name of Christ is to exercise what we have chosen to call a community-building ministry. It is a ministry that requires not only a continual openness to the Spirit, but sensitivity, wisdom, and skill.

II
COMMUNITY BUILDING
IN THE WORLD AT LARGE

The primary focus for a community-building ministry is within the structures of society, depending, of course, on where we have or can gain access. It could involve working to heal brokenness within a family, either our own or someone else's. It could mean involvement with the acute problems of global injustice, the gap between the "haves" and the "have nots." In order to create a more equitable world community, Dag Hammarskjold, the late Secretary General of the United

Nations, set out to build an organization that would be responsive not only to the superpowers, but to those newly emerging nations that were struggling for survival. Hammarskjold conceived of what he was doing as a calling, a response to the work of the Spirit. As James McLendon writes, his "success was intimately linked with an interiority, a discipline, a vision which was formed by the gospel of the cross, a vision which found in Jesus, and in the way of sacrifice, and in the mystical apprehension beyond the frontiers of the unheard-of, models for self-knowledge, images for action, which made that life possible."[3] In Dag Hammarskjold a community-building ministry to the world was hammered out through political persuasion and organizational change.

For a number of years an ecumenical group known as Metropolitan Associates of Philadelphia (MAP) worked at developing support groups for laity engaged in community-building ministries within large organizations.[4] In a series of seminars, MAP helped people identify the varieties of ministries available to the laity of the church and then move toward an examination of how ministries of change can be exercised in large organizations. Strategies for these particular ministries were worked out in support groups of men and women who met on a weekly basis to help identify possibilities and evaluate results. In one instance, an employee of a paper company helped to tackle a problem of declining morale within his office that had emerged as a result of what many felt was an arbitrary decision on the part of management. In a similar project, several couples organized themselves to tackle a problem of increased juvenile crime. Theirs was a long-term ministry that began in response to a need and ended in a major program involving an entire community. In both cases, the emphasis was not simply on solving a problem or making life more pleasant, but on the clear intent to act in a particular situation in the name of Christ. At every step along the way they took time to study the Scriptures to find what they were being called to do.

In a project aimed at developing a more mutual sense of ministry within the life of the parish, a group of eight persons (including the clergy) from two New England congregations met weekly for three months to see if they could identify the nature of the ministry to which each person had been called. They worked primarily with pre-selected case studies in an effort to see how ministry could be carried out in a variety of settings. Eventually persons were writing their own case studies based on experiences at work or in the community at large. The questions they addressed were: "What kind of ministry needs to be exercised here?" and "What are the resources of faith that I can draw on to give me direction and strength?"

Community-building ministries in society take countless forms. They can be highly individualized or else organized into tightly disciplined "mission groups" aimed at addressing a particular problem. Whatever the focus, to be sustained ministry must involve support, personal reflection, and a meditative study of Scripture. A typical format for a ministry development group might go like this:

1.A half hour of Bible study prepared for ahead of time. (The Acts of the Apostles is a good place to begin.)

2.A half hour in which participants can share how they have been involved in ministry during the past week.

3.An hour's discussion in response to a case study or problem situation prepared by a member. The purpose of this is both to provide support and to help clarify possibilities. Normally, the person who is "up front" presents his or her situation and then remains quiet for fifteen minutes while others react. The questions might be: "What is happening here?" "What are the tensions or block to community?" "What kind of ministry is being called for?" "How might we go about it?" After the fifteen minutes are up, the presenter joins the discussion as it moves to draw on the resources of faith that are available.

Community-building ministries are needed to help maintain the often delicate balances which exist within family life. They are needed in industry and government both locally and on the world scene. They can be as sophisticated as a Dag Hammarskjold or as simple as helping a person in need. Our task is to develop the discipline and the skill—the ability to listen, to organize, to problem-solve, to build trust—so that Christ can use us as instruments of healing and reconciliation.

We do not create community; it is the work of the Spirit. It happens when people and groups are released from the bondage of their boxes. We can, however, share in the process, being open to the possibilities that God does indeed present to us. The task of the Church is to help people identify what these ministries might be and then to provide support for those called to carry them out.

III
COMMUNITY BUILDING WITHIN THE CHURCH

The call to help build human community involves the Christian, not only with the structures of society but also with that community of faith from which we are given direction and support. From those first days after Pentecost, Christians have met together to hear the apostolic teaching—The Story —"to share the common life, to break bread, and to pray" (Acts 2:42). The sign of their fellowship in Christ was their capacity to care for one another. Koinonia is a description of a community where people, energized by the love of God, care for one another. A congregation is a place of support because it is a place where we can legitimately expect that at least some people are concerned about our well-being. A congregation is by its very calling a community of love, accountability, and support. To the degree that this fails to be true, there is every reason for disillusionment.

Every congregation, therefore, must have within its membership a group of persons committed to a community-building ministry within the congregation itself. Such a ministry should be self-conscious and rooted in an ongoing discipline. It could involve visiting the sick and shut-ins, staying in touch with the membership, and reaching out to newcomers or fringe members in an effort to include them in the common life of the congregation. Such a ministry would also include addressing those points where tension has arisen in an effort to find resolution before dislocation occurs. This kind of ministry, normally shared with the clergy, is of critical importance to the life of a congregation and needs to be approached with maturity and skill. It involves being able to surface conflict (and not bury it) and then working for its resolution. Such a vision emerges from an order model of community, but takes seriously the role of conflict in opening up new possibilities for growth.

Not long ago I was asked to meet with members of a small rural congregation about training for lay ministry. From the very beginning of our first session, however, it was obvious that there was another agenda of more pressing importance. With the support and encouragement of the pastor, a group had developed within the congregation who were committed to a charismatic approach to the Christian life. Although professing their openness and love for their brothers and sisters, the group communicated to others a sense of elitism that was highly divisive.

Scrapping the original design, we spent the day developing a strategy by which the church could deal with this highly volatile conflict by actually working on the conflict ourselves. Participants were asked to write anonymously what they saw the problem to be and how they were affected by it personally. I then collected the statements and read them out while someone else wrote them on the board. We spent time reacting to these statements, seeing if we could identify the conflicting points of view. In this case two seemed most obvious. I then asked for two volunteers to role-play a position other than their own, each having the task of explaining to the other how he thought and felt (in role). After some hesitation, two volunteers stepped forward and we went at it for five minutes. I then stopped the action and asked how the participants felt. "Peculiar," said one. "I'm getting slightly different ideas about how those people feel," said the other, although he let it be known he was not convinced. I then asked them to switch roles and play their own position. We did this for five minutes, reflected a bit, and then reversed again. After this was over and the role-players were debriefed (most important!), we shared what we had learned about the feelings and convictions that underlay the conflict. At this point we were ready to suggest some possible strategies for resolving what was potentially a highly explosive situation.

This design is relatively simple; it can be carried out by anyone who is not emotionally involved in the conflict and who is trusted by those who are. It is based on several assumptions about the nature of conflict that are worth noting.

1.Conflict is always present within persons, between persons, and between persons and organizations, and therefore needs to be recognized and responded to creatively.

2.It is better to focus on what people are trying to accomplish than why they are acting the way they do.

3.Clarification of goals tends to make conflict more public and sometimes more intense, but it is a necessary step toward resolution.

4.Persons and organizations need an adequate psychological power base in order to respond to conflict creatively. We can help this by affirming people's worth even when disagreeing with the position.

5.There needs to be an adequate relational base among persons and sufficient openness to respond to conflict creatively. I need to experience something of what you are feeling.

6.Creative communication (testing assumptions and listening reflectively) is essential.

7.More than one solution needs to be examined and tested.

8.To be effective, conflict management processes must be institutionalized and not created for special occasions.[5]

I am convinced that if we are serious about Christian community, we need to raise up persons within the life of the congregation who can help in the resolution of conflict. Nothing is more destructive to congregational life than the inability to deal with conflict creatively, which, unfortunately, is more the pattern than the exception.

One other aspect of a community-building ministry is worth noting, both because of its importance and because it is so often neglected in the so-called mainline churches. This is the ministry to the lapsed and unchurched, aimed at building up (enlarging) the community of faith. Just because we are often repelled by methods used by some churches, we are not therefore relieved of the responsibility of developing other methods that meet criteria consistent with what we believe. We are told in Acts of that first Christian community that "day by day the Lord added to their number those whom he was saving" (Acts 2:47). This did not occur by accident. It happened because the church worked at enlarging its membership both without hesitation and without apology.

In a little book entitled *How To Grow a Church*, which comes out of the conservative evangelical tradition, the authors rightly point to the question of attitude as the key issue that a congregation must face. "If the Church is preaching the good news of God's power to needy people, if it is *concerned* about church growth, if it is *thinking* about church growth, if it is *praying* about church growth, if it *enlists* people in the growth of the church, there is no reason why it shouldn't grow. You see, God wants his children found."[6] There is added to this affirmation, however, the necessity for setting long- and short-range growth goals, training in this kind of ministry, and an educational program that not only makes growth acceptable but strengthens the capacity of a congregation to receive new members. There are obvious dangers in an uncritical commitment to numerical growth. Big is not necessarily best. The issue, however, is our responsibility to the Gospel itself. If the church is a source of life, then we have a responsibility to share with others, with authenticity and integrity, what we ourselves have been given.

Community-building within the congregation involves both the quality of congregational life and a clearly articulated ministry to the unchurched. It involves taking seriously the psychological contracts people make with a congregation— their underlying expectations—and creating programs and groupings that respond to genuine need. In a fascinating book entitled *The Apathetic and Bored Church Member*,[7] John Savage points out that much of what we write off as disinterest on the part of lapsed members has its base in intense anxiety. In interviewing twenty-three persons, all of whom had been inactive in the church for some time, Savage discovered that no one had ever inquired of any of the twenty-three why they had lost interest or dropped out. They had simply dropped away unnoticed, reinforcing their belief that people did not care and that they had not been missed. Several other findings in this study are of particular importance to a community-building ministry:

•In every case, some incident precipitated the drop-out.

•The first two months after people had dropped away from worship was the critical time for recovery.

•After this time other involvements had begun to form, usually involving the family.

•The precipitating events, when church-centered, involved conflict with the clergy or other members of the congregation, feelings of overwork, physical trauma, moral anxiety, neurotic or existential anxiety.

•Eighty percent of those visited returned to church life.

Community building is a ministry of many dimensions and many skills. It lies at the heart of what it means to be the Church.

IV

"Prayer is the language of Christian community," writes Henri Nouwen. "In prayer the nature of the community becomes visible because in prayer we direct ourselves to the one who forms the community. We do not pray to each other, but together we pray to God, who calls us and makes us a new people."[8] It is in the act of worship that we experience the gift of community at its deepest level. In the eucharistic offering of bread and wine, our brokenness and separation are offered in symbolic union with the broken body of Christ, and then given back transformed and made whole as a sign of that new community brought into being by his resurrection. If we are to understand what it means to be community-builders, we must do so from this perspective. Ministry is given to us by God. It remains authentic only as it is empowered at its source, supported and guided by the community of faith, and then shared with others. "Make me an instrument of your peace," prayed St. Francis. "Where there is hatred, let me sow love; where there is injury, pardon; where there is discord, union." This is what it means to exercise a community-building ministry, to be in the fullest sense, an ambassador of reconciliation.

CHAPTER VI

A Disciplined Journey

*After this he went journeying
from town to town and village to
village, proclaiming the good news
of the kingdom of God."*

LUKE 8:1

I

The image of the journey has been a familiar one within
Christian literature. Be it the story of *Pilgrim's Progress* or the
orthodox classic, *The Way of the Pilgrim,* the description of a
serious quest for faith seems best couched in the context of
disciplined movement. Our prototype, of course, is the patri-
arch Abraham. Called from familiar surroundings to an unknown land, he set out, we are told, without delay. His response was an act of faith, a self-conscious offering of his
future to the God of Promise. His journey, therefore, was
primarily a journey of the Spirit. The idea of a spiritual journey refers to that movement of the Spirit within the human
psyche—that inner journey—which results in the unfolding
of those limitless possibilities implanted within us at birth.
The journey of the human spirit is an image of growth. It is
a description of our quest for wholeness by which, through
God's grace, we become what we were created to be.

The Christian journey is an act of discipline taken on in
response to the love of God made known to us in Jesus Christ.
It is, therefore, a profound act of ministry. It is a disciplined

attempt to bear witness to who Christ is by taking seriously
who *we* are. The Christian journey implies the living of our
lives in such a way that Christ can be formed in us. It has little
to do with special acts of public piety, as worthwhile as these
may be, but the decision to live out our lives as authentically
as possible in the name of Christ.

II

In the pages that follow I would like to describe four elements that I am convinced are necessary for undertaking the
Christian Journey in today's world. They are:

Harmony
Grounding
Solitude
Compassion

Without these elements incorporated into our lives, we soon
become more wanderers than journeyers. They are the elements by which our journeys are nourished and given direction. "With deep roots and firm foundations," writes the author of Ephesians, we are called to grasp "what is the breadth
and length and height and depth of the love of Christ, and to
know it, though it is beyond knowledge. So may you attain to
fullness of being, the fullness of God himself" (Eph 3:18, 19).

Harmony

If we are serious about the Christian journey, the place to
begin is not with how we say our prayers but with how we
spend our time. The Christian journey is a focused use of life
energy. Our aim is to discover the kind of harmony that reflects the humanity of Christ and, therefore, the best humanity
that is in ourselves. Dr. Bryan Hall suggests that we characteristically expend life energy in four ways—through *work,*

through personal and social *maintenance,* through *play,* and through what he calls *"freesense."*[1]

Work, for most of us, is the cornerstone of the life experience if for no other reason than the fact that it involves the major part of the time available to us. From the time we begin school, a great deal of energy is invested in what might normally be defined as work—the act of coping, doing, or producing. When we expend energy in work with minimal satisfaction, it affects our spiritual growth just as radically as the way we pray. In this sense, work is more than a job for which we are paid, it has to do with the way we expend our creative energy for the completion of a task. When the sense of completion is frustrated, or when creativity is replaced by compulsiveness (working to escape some other area of life or to prove our worth), our life is out of harmony.

Maintenance, on the other hand, uses life energy in a quite different way. It has to do with the way we care for ourselves and the way we care for others. When we abuse our bodies by overwork, overeating, or overdrinking, we throw our lives out of harmony. In the same sense, if all our relationships are maintained out of a sense of "ought" or ritualized to the point of emptiness, the life energy available for authentic maintenance is thwarted. Maintenance is a major part of everyone's life. We expend life energy maintaining friendships, caring for children, or simply engaging other persons in the course of a day's work. The time we spend on maintenance and the quality of the relationships we enjoy are critical questions to consider in our spiritual journeys, for they reflect the balance and authenticity of the way we live.

Play, Hall's third category, is distinctly different. It involves those expressions of fantasy or imagination or just plain fun, when we experience ourselves to be beyond obligation. Although we desperately need to play, we never play because we have to. Play is more spontaneous and free, be it in athletic endeavor or simply in running down a hill in wild abandon. It is a time when the child in us is affirmed and given reign. In this sense, play stands in juxtaposition to work and maintenance. It involves using life energy in a different way.

Freesense might well be thought of as the deeper side of play. It involves those moments when we are sufficiently in touch with ourselves to be "wholly present" to someone else. Freesense is a description of those experiences which open us to the transcendent dimension of life, whether while listening to a Beethoven symphony or in the awareness of the presence of God which comes in meditation. Freesense is something which permeates every thing we do. Although we arrange our life in such a way as to insure time for freesense, when cultivated, freesense will also be a part of our work, our maintenance, and our play. When work involves strong elements of freesense, it becomes what we generally call vocation. Or when play involves freesense, it takes on that quality we refer to as "celebration." Freesense is a description of that state in which it is possible for the "I" to encounter the "Thou."

For most people play and freesense are rare experiences. Their life energy is spent to a large degree in work and maintenance, leaving little left for anything else. On a retreat for a religious order of women, everyone was asked to analyze how they had spent their time during the past month. Percentages were assigned to each of the four categories as calendars were reviewed. Ten out of fourteen persons present noted that they were in the forty percent range for work, forty-five percent for maintenance, five percent for play, and ten percent for freesense. The time set apart for play generally turned out to be more maintenance than play, more like "working" at play than actually playing. Others identified how often it was that the time of prayer, an opportunity for freesense, was more often burdened with a sense of "ought." No wonder! There was no energy available for prayer; it was all used up on work and maintenance. Their lives were out of harmony.

The Christian journey is a journey toward wholeness. It is what we might call an adventure in spiritual growth. To talk about spiritual growth, however, is to talk about all of life. Spiritual growth involves not only the way we "pray" but the way we "play." It is concerned with harmony, the balanced use of life energy in a way that the whole person is nourished by the Spirit of God. Harmony emerges when work, maintenance, play, and freesense are held together in realistic balance.

Grounding

The Christian journey is not a journey from somewhere to nowhere. It is a journey from self-awareness to an ever-deepening communion with God, expressed in an ever-deepening compassion for the world. It is a journey in which our own unfolding story becomes more and more in tune with the biblical story of redemption. It is essential, therefore, that our journey be grounded in the tradition from which it draws life.

In his introduction to the book, *Sacred Tradition and Present Need*, Jacob Needleman makes an interesting observation about the spiritual climate currently present in the United States. "The current spiritual ferment in California epitomizes the yearning of twentieth-century man for catalytic answers to the fundamental question of existence," he writes. "The new religions experiment with meditation and other religious techniques; attempts at self-exploration and human relations through sensory awareness, encounter, and communes have now spread throughout the world." All this, however, poses a serious question: "Has the spiritual revolution lost its direction in a profusion of innovation?" Needleman asks, "In our haste to reject our worn religious forms, customs and ideals, have we overlooked the truths that have guided traditional life and thought since time immemorial?"[2]

I find this question to be of profound importance. My own spiritual journey has been immeasurably enriched by the innovation of which Needleman speaks, but I have also discovered that the deeper I enter into the process of my own journey, the deeper is the yearning for a fresh encounter with the tradition in which my journey was born. For me, therefore, the need to ground one's journey within the flow of sacred tradition is a matter of genuine seriousness. Without this we become dilettantes of the spiritual life, tasting here and nibbling there, but never taking the ultimate leap of faith. I am a Christian both by birth and by choice. It is in the continuous rediscovery of the depths of this tradition that my journey is both grounded and given life.

In grounding my own journey, there are four anchors that I have found to be central and therefore particularly helpful. They are: (1) regular participation in the corporate worship of the community of faith; (2) study and reflection—attempting to strike some balance between the study of Scripture and reading in the classics of the Christian spiritual tradition, as well as ongoing encounters with current writing that squarely confront me with the pain of the world; (3) the support of an ongoing group of people with whom I can share my journey, and; 4) a spiritual guide or director.

Let us look first at the subject of worship. The Christian journey is something quite different from the popular "do your own thing." It is as intensely *corporate* as it is intensely *personal.* In the worship of the Christian community the story of redemption is recalled, remembered, and entered into. Although ideally there is a strong sense of community, there is also an element of awe and timelessness. We are responding to symbols that echo the great archetypes of human existence: bread and wine, death and resurrection, guilt and forgiveness; symbols that empower and shape our stories in what we see and hear and feel in those levels of comprehension far beneath the level of consciousness. The Christian journey is one undertaken in the company of other pilgrims. In the act of worship, therefore, we take our place with all who undertake the journey—both the living and the dead—that our common humanity might be lifted up as one joyous act of praise.

A second anchor on which to ground the Christian journey is the discipline of regular study. Such study would naturally involve an ongoing and critical exploration of the Bible. In this way we are widening the resources available to us in meditation, as well as tilling the soil so the seeds of our journey might grow. For the sake of balance, however, reading should also involve opportunities for serious reflection on contemporary culture, for through the events that surround us we are also confronted and nourished by the Word of God.

There is a third category of material, however, that is not generally known to those just beginning their journey. These are the classics of the Christian Spiritual tradition that have been passed down through the centuries. Although these mystical classics have been continually reprinted, they are virtually unknown to the vast number of persons who look to the Church as their spiritual home. We have available to us the inner experiences of other journeyers like ourselves, whose writings are part of the treasures we share. As a start, *The Way of the Pilgrim* and *Writings From the Philokolia* are doorways into the heritage of Eastern Christianity, and such classics as St. Teresa's *The Interior Castle*, the anonymous *Cloud of Unknowing*, and the *Confessions of Jacob Boehme* would be good points of entry into the West. In reading the literature of the past some adaptation is necessary, although not as much as we might suspect. When St. Teresa describes what it is like to experience God at the deepest level of her being, she is addressing the most contemporary of persons.

Our third anchor is a relationship to a group of people who

are willing to meet regularly for mutual encouragement and support. Journey groups are more than an occasional meeting of friends. They are intentional gatherings, on at least a monthly basis, of six to twelve persons whose primary *raison d'etre* is to support each other in their spiritual journey. The ongoing agenda for such a group will vary from place to place, but it will include some opportunity to share with each other where we have been, where we believe ourselves to be, and where we see ourselves moving. One such journey group meets every three weeks for an hour and a half. Their time together includes Bible study, mutual sharing of common concerns, and then serious work in ways in which individuals can simplify their style of life. Quite obviously, other groups have other concerns. The secret of longevity lies in meeting on a regular basis for a common purpose.

The fourth anchor for grounding the Christian journey reaches back to the earliest days of the Christian experience. It is a discipline normally referred to as *spiritual direction,* a serious relationship between two persons where one agrees to help guide the other on his journey. Henri Nouwen writes that "a careful look at the lives of people for whom prayer was indeed 'the only thing needed' [see Luke 10:42] shows that three 'rules' are always observed: a contemplative reading of the word of God, a silent listening to the voice of God, and a trusting obedience to a spiritual guide."[3] I prefer the word "guidance" to the more traditional word "direction" simply because it places the emphasis on collegiality rather than on a defined structure of authority. It is my dream that the day will soon come when spiritual guidance will be common practice within the Christian community. It is an opportunity for one journeyer to help another become clearer about the direction of his life and provide support in dealing with the obstacles that get in the way. Some guides are more experienced than others, and there are times in our journey that we need more experienced help. This does not, however, negate the necessity of spiritual companions along the way, persons who share our commitment to a disciplined journey, who are able to listen to us with an inner ear, and who are willing to place their experience at our disposal.

Spiritual guidance is not therapy, nor is it the giving of advice. Its aim is to provide assistance in both clarification and discernment. It involves sitting down on a regular basis with someone you trust in order to examine, adjust, and recommit yourself to the disciplines that give substance to your journey. It might be that your spiritual guide is someone you do not normally see, but from whom you feel you will gain wisdom. Or it might be that you find a person who is a spiritual companion to you at the same time that you are a spiritual companion to him. It is incidental whether the relationship lasts a year or a lifetime. The important thing is that the relationship be one in which you are able to talk comfortably and reflectively about the unfolding process of your spiritual journey, knowing that it is in the living out of this spiritual journey that Christ is made known through you to others.

Solitude

"Our language has wisely sensed two sides of man's being alone," Paul Tillich once wrote. "It has created the word 'loneliness' to express the *pain* of being alone, and it has created the word 'solitude' to express the *glory* of being alone."[4] It is in embracing solitude that our spiritual journey moves from the surface to the depths. We embrace solitude through prayer. Prayer is our access to the mystery of life which lies just beyond our vision. At its deepest level it is not something we do but something which the Holy Spirit does in us and through us. To say that we "ought" to pray is like saying we ought to breathe. No one would dispute it; it just feels like a case of misplaced emphasis. Prayer is as natural a part of the life process as breathing. It is the avenue to those deep places within ourselves where the Spirit is encountered.

For many people today, prayer is a stumbling block to the Christian journey. They see it as "magic" on the one hand, or as essentially meaningless on the other. "I know I ought to pray, but . . ." is a phrase often repeated by persons who in all other respects are quite serious about the quality of their spiritual journey. Prayer becomes a difficulty when, first of all, it is separated from our ongoing quest for wholeness (it becomes "spooky"); and secondly, when it becomes overly dependent on words (talk becomes a substitute for depth). The Christian journey is an ongoing process by which we learn to make solitude our friend. There are four elements in this process that I have found especially helpful. The first has to do with keeping a daily journal of our inner life. The second, mastering the art of "centering"—entering into the stillness. Thirdly, we move from the "centered" state to meditation itself. And finally, we find that our meditation begins to move us beyond words—contemplation. When all four of these elements are woven together in an ongoing spiritual discipline, we find that solitude is as necessary for us as the air we breathe.

First of all, a word about keeping a journal. A journal can be as elaborate or as simple as we desire to make it. It is the means by which we record the process of our inner journey. It can include a brief description of our dreams, notes on the content of meditation, particular feelings or insights that occurred during the day, or simply things we noticed or read that we want to record. Dr. Ira Progoff, the founder of Dialogue House in New York, has developed journal keeping into a profound psychological art which he describes fully in his *At a Journal Workshop*,[5] but for most people, journal keeping will begin on a simpler plane.

The theological affirmation underlying journal writing is

the conviction that our encounter with God is essentially dialogical. Just as God encounters us externally through people and events, he encounters us internally through memories, images, or the stories that constitute the movement of our lives. Spiritual growth involves conscious participation in this dialogue, both with others (sharing) and within ourselves (solitude). The journal makes it possible to listen and reflect upon this dialogue as it unfolds through the process of our lives. One of the secrets to keeping a journal is to make an entry each day, even if you do nothing more than record the date, and then, at least on a monthly basis, read it over and let its content become the subject of your meditation.

Secondly, the art of centering. For those brought up in the Quaker tradition, "centering" is a familiar term. To "center down" means to turn off external stimuli so that you could begin to listen with an inner ear. Centering is a skill we can learn. It involves an increasing capacity for "passive concentration" where, instead of concentrating with an intense act of will, we bring into focus the energy already present within us. The increasing interest in the great Eastern religions which we now see in this country has made us acutely aware of the importance of breathing in the centering process. Breathing, in Eastern thought, is more than concern for the air which fills the lungs. Through attention to the pattern of our breathing, we are able to enter into harmony with the rhythm of the cosmos. This same concept is emphasized in our own tradition with the use of the Jesus Prayer, so popular in Eastern Christianity. This is a meditation in which the words of prayer— "Lord Jesus Christ, Son of God, have mercy upon me"—are united with the rhythm of breathing, so that we literally pray as we breathe. The centering process, however, can be wordless. It is the basic skill necessary for the inner journey.

The obvious fruit of the centering process is an increased capacity for meditation. Indeed, many would say, the process of centering is itself a form of meditation. Meditation is a word used to describe many paths—some closely tied to the religious experience of humankind, others more secular and psychological. At its core, however, meditation refers to the discipline of sustained reflection aimed at increased inner concentration. To use Claudio Naranjo's words, it is "concerned with the development of a *presence*, a modality of being, which may be expressed or developed in whatever situation the individual may be involved."[6] In Christian terminology, however, meditation has most often been understood as dwelling on certain words or ideas, usually inspired by the Scriptures. In this sense, it is different from what is referred to as "contemplation," where the mind and heart are focused on the mystery of God that lies beyond words. "Meditation investigates," writes Richard of St. Victor, "contemplation wonders."[7] In most of the Eastern traditions, the word "meditation" is used to describe both of these experiences.

The content of meditation can come from a biblical passage or from a concept such as the love of God. The idea is to take whatever thoughts or images emerge and let them speak to us in the silence. By focusing on the Gospel, it is possible to enter into dialogue with the person of Christ. When this becomes a regular practice, the substance of this dialogue becomes more and more integrated with other aspects of our thought. The secret of meditation is regularity, be it five or thirty minutes a day. The more regular our discipline becomes, the deeper the process goes. Meditation opens up the dark corners of our psyche to the light of the Spirit. We can encounter events and persons in our past, "wisdom figures" who have influenced the direction of our journey or who are integral to the biblical story, for it is through all these situations and people that God speaks.

Meditation, when practiced regularly in dialogue with the

Holy Spirit invariably leads us to that encounter with the Divine Presence that is essentially wordless, or beyond the images we normally associate with thought. In traditional Christian terminology, this is called contemplation. Contemplation is more intuitive than rational. It is, in Thomas Merton's words, "a response to a call: a call from Him Who has no voice, and yet Who speaks in everything that is, and Who, most of all, speaks in the depths of our being: for we ourselves are words of His." "Contemplation," he continues, "is this echo."[8]

I am convinced that the Christian journey will never expand to the dimensions open to it until we are able to adopt, in those ways that are unique to each of us, what we might best call a "contemplative life style." We are not referring here to life in a monastery (although for a very few that might be included) but for a way of life which seeks to cultivate a deep and ongoing awareness of the person of Christ. It is a way of life that is increasingly aware of both the depths in one's self and the depth in others. It is a vision of life permeated with the love of God.

Compassion

If solitude is the doorway through which we enter into our own story, compassion is the doorway into the world's story and the two stories are intimately related. The great truth of the spiritual life is that the more we enter into the depths of our own being, the more related we become to the world around us. The quality and intensity of this relatedness to the larger world is the true test of the quality of our inner journey. "There is no true solitude except interior solitude," writes Thomas Merton. "And interior solitude is not possible for anyone who does not accept his right place in relation to other men. There is no true peace possible for the man who still imagines that some accident of talent or grace or virtue segregates him from other men and places him above them. Solitude is not separation."⁹

One of the fruits of solitude is an increased capacity for compassion—the ability "to suffer with" another's pain. It comes about as the result of an increased sense of solidarity with the human family of which we are a part. When Paul talks about "suffering with those who suffer," he is talking about compassion, that supreme gift without which we are less than fully human. It might well be that the greatest threat to human survival now confronting us is not the loss of energy or the increase of pollution, but the loss of compassion. We are confronted daily with the pain of human tragedy—the breakup of a family or the sunken face of a starving child—to such an extent that we soon learn to turn off what we see. In order to cope with our feelings of helplessness, we teach ourselves how *not* to feel. The tragedy in this response, which is probably more widespread than we dare believe, is that we also deaden our capacity for love. For Christians, the cross stands as an ever-present reminder that love and suffering are two sides of the same coin.

We have been speaking of four elements that seem to be necessary for the Christian journey: harmony, grounding, solitude and compassion. There is no order of priority in these as all are closely interrelated. Without one, the others are incomplete. Compassion is the gift by which we move from being passive respondents to the flood of events that make up the human story, to being participants with Christ in healing the world's pain. If compassion is often thwarted by a sense of helplessness, then it is important to incorporate in our journey ways in which we can act, even if on a minute scale. There are four ways that come immediately to mind that seem worth such incorporation. They are: (1) the development of a global awareness; (2) the increase of our capacity to be "present" with others; (3) the inclusion in our spiritual disciplines of specific intercessions for those in need; and (4) The creation of settings for what might best be called "focused caring."

First of all, the development of a global awareness. Ira Progoff writes of the experience of entering into the depths of one's own psyche to discover there an underground stream in which all humanity is gathered.[10] The experience of entering into that stream carries with it an awareness that we are indissolubly bound up with all humankind in a network of interconnectedness. This sense of interconnectedness is a sign of spiritual maturity. It seems to be a common experience that the more deeply we encounter the divine presence within ourselves, the more profound is our sense of oneness with those in need. The suffering of Christ continues in the suffering of mankind. The brokenness and separation of the human family—indeed of the entire created order—reflects the brokenness of Christ's own body. To use an image of Thomas Merton's, the love of God involves us in the suffering of the world because it is the aim of God's love to reset the broken bones of humanity. Global awareness, then, is the awareness of the profound interconnectedness of the created order. It is the awareness within ourselves that the agony of racial violence is our agony, whether it occurs in the United States or Africa. It is the awareness that when a stream is polluted, or when one human being is demeaned by another, something inside us is also polluted or demeaned. Global awareness is the simple recognition that "we are relatives all." It is the first step toward genuine compassion.

Another aspect of compassion is the ability to *be present* to someone else. The word "present" is used here in a special sense. It is used to describe a relationship in which my capacity for hearing, seeing, feeling—indeed, loving—is made available to another human being if only for a moment. To be present to another person means that I have in a particular moment dared to move beyond my protective armor and allowed myself to be vulnerable.

One of the dangers of a disciplined journey is that we become so intent on the form of the journey that we lose touch with the substance. In the name of Christ, we become so adept at helping others that the very act of helping becomes a screen which prevents genuine human encounter. A daily discipline, a clear sense of direction, even an intense consciousness of Christ are of little use if they do not enable us to be more authentic persons. Authenticity involves not only being able to give help to others but being able to ask for it for ourselves, not only giving love but receiving it. Being present to another person is an expression of freesense, spoken of earlier. It is a moment of transcendence when the Spirit overcomes the separation that is both within us, and between us and another. As Henri Nouwen writes, "Love not only lasts forever, it needs only a second to come about."[11]

A third way in which compassion is developed and increased is by intercession, or praying for others. It is a way of reaching beyond time and geography to hold in our vision some person or persons, known or unknown, that they may experience the life-giving energy of God, energy that moves from us through God to them. "It is impossible for one individual to be involved on all levels and at all points of the compass at the same time," writes Brother Pierre-Yves Emery of the Taizé community in France. "This is another limit to our presence with others. But other persons become committed where I am not, and they do what I cannot do . . . So relying on the limited but serious involvement that is properly mine, my prayer can legitimately reach out to emergencies and needs in areas where other men and women are striving to bring answers. In unity with God's plan, intercession makes me more acutely, more newly conscious of the unity of all people on Earth, and of that unity which is the communion of saints in Christ—unity in misfortune and need, but also unity in service and commitment."[12]

In the early days of my ministry, I was taught something about intercession that I have never forgotten. I was visiting an elderly woman dying of cancer. Despite all the medication she had been given, her pain was apparent. Aware of my discomfort, this very wise and caring lady said this to me, "It is not pain I most fear. It is the feeling of uselessness. The greatest help you can be to me is to bring me names of people who are in desperate need. I am learning to offer my pain with the suffering of Christ for specific people. This way, I don't feel useless. It's a way of putting all that happens to me to some useful purpose." Here in the still vital life of a dying woman was compassion expressed through intercession. She died shortly after this visit, but the power of her journey is to this day a very present reality, not only to me but to the people who knew her and to the people for whom she prayed.

The final aspect of compassion, which I found in my own life to be important, is what I call *focused caring*. The dying woman who taught me the meaning of intercession was engaged in focused caring. Instead of caring for the world and accomplishing nothing, she focused her energies in such a way that there was a sense of purposefulness in what she did. The more aware we become of the range of human need that surrounds us, the more overwhelmed we can become, to the point that we end up doing nothing. The secret of the compassionate life is to focus our care on a few things that we can do something about, including in our intercessions those concerns that are beyond our reach. I know of one person who chose to focus all of his energy on dealing with the problem of Vietnamese refugees. He stayed with this until he felt he had made some genuine contribution, resisting the sometimes angry entreaties of friends to take on things which, to them, were more urgent. The ability to bring into focus the energy we expend

is of critical importance to the Christian journey. It allows us
to give to others without losing touch with ourselves. It re-
minds us that we are finite, with the freedom to say no as well
as yes in the recognition that our particular gifts can be used
in some ways better than others.

III

The Christian disciple is called to undertake a disciplined
journey, a journey inward and a journey outward. It is this
journey that not only gives a sense of meaning and direction
in life, it is itself a ministry, a way of proclaiming to the world
the "unsearchable riches of Christ." We proclaim what we
live. The Christian journey is a life lived from inside out, a life
in which the things we experience within—dreams, memories, images, and symbols, and the presence of him whom we
encounter in the deep silence—are in constant tension and
dialogue with all that we experience without—people, events,
joys, sorrows, and the presence of him whom we encounter in
others. Thomas Merton repeats a suggestion of Douglas Steere
that the absence of this tension might well produce the most
pervasive form of violence present in contemporary society.
"To allow one's self to be carried away by a multitude of
conflicting concerns," Merton writes, "to surrender to too
many demands, to commit one's self to too many projects, to
want to help everyone in everything is to succumb to violence.
Frenzy destroys our inner capacity for peace. It destroys the
fruitfulness of our work, because it kills the root of inner
wisdom which makes work fruitful."[13]

One of the most critical tasks of the local church is to enable
people to become "journeyers" rather than "wanderers." This
suggests that the leadership of a congregation needs to be
serious about their own journeys, to the point where they are
willing to share their experience with others, not as those who

have arrived but as fellow journeyers able to receive as well as to give. Congregations are the natural settings for training in the contemplative disciplines, as well as the settings in which groups might form to give direction and support along the way. For most congregations, it will mean a reordering of priorities for the development of a step-by-step strategy for the cultivation and nurture of a disciplined apostolate committed to the exercises of Christ's ministry in the world.

In his *Markings,* Dag Hammarskjold records some of the often agonizing turning points that were the occasion of the deepening of his remarkable journey. One entry in this journal describes with particular wisdom that sense of creative tension which is the mark of wholeness. "The more faithfully you listen to the voice within you," he writes, "the better you will hear what is sounding outside. And only he who listens can speak. In this the starting of the road toward the union of your two dreams—to be allowed in clarity of mind to mirror life, and in purity of heart to mold it?"[14] Ultimately, this is the question we all must ask, for it is the question Christ asks of us.

CHAPTER VII

The Ministry of Enablement

And these were his gifts: some to be apostles, some prophets, some evangelists, some pastors and teachers, to equip God's people for work in his service, to the building up of the body of Christ.

EPHESIANS 4:11–14

"The word 'enablement,' is related to the word 'ministry.' " This is an expression that has deep theological roots. It suggests not only a function but an ethos in which this function is carried out. The ministry of enablement is a crucial element in the ongoing renewal of the life of the local congregation. It is also, despite our best intentions, quite difficult to practice.

The concept of "ministry as enablement" is firmly rooted in the New Testament understanding of the Church's mission. The way in which Jesus empowered his disciples for their ministry had the effect of enabling them to exercise ministries that built on the unique gifts which each possessed. The phrase, "And he began to teach them," recurs again and again. "Come with me, by yourselves, to some place where you can rest quietly," Jesus said to his disciples as he enabled them to find inner nourishment for what they were being asked to do (Mk 8). "After this," Luke records, "the Lord appointed a further seventy-two and sent them on ahead in pairs to every town and place he was going to visit himself" (Lk 10:1). These were all enabling functions, crucial to our understanding of the task of the Church.

It is in the Epistle to the Ephesians, however, that our charge is most clearly stated. "And these were his gifts," states the writer, "some to be apostles, some prophets, some evangelists, some pastors and teachers, to equip God's people for work in his service, to the building up of the body of Christ" (Eph 4:11–14). The task of the Church's ministry is to equip one another so that all might live as Christ's servants in the world. The key word is "equip," which in its root form refers to the "building up" of the body, the community of faith, and the "spiritual strengthening necessary for the 'service of Christ' in the world." The word "enablement" has a similar meaning, although coming from a different root. Enablement refers to the process by which we make it possible for others to find both the strength and authority to fulfill the purposes of their lives. As the *laos*—the people of God ordained and not ordained—we have been sent into the world to exercise ministry according to the gifts given us by the Spirit. As Paul wrote to the church in Corinth, "you possess full knowledge and you can give full expression to it. . . . There is indeed no single gift you lack, while you wait expectantly for our Lord Jesus Christ to reveal himself" (1 Cor. 1:6–7). Every member of the body possesses the gifts necessary for ministry. The task of the congregation, therefore, is to enable these gifts to be put to use. We are a community of people gathered by the Spirit to proclaim and celebrate Christ's redeeming activity in the world. We exist not for ourselves, but on behalf of the world of which we are a part. The process by which men, women, and children are enabled to exercise ministry, both within the community and in society at large, is fundamental to who we are. The way we organize to perform our task, therefore, is a question of crucial importance.

II

Several years ago an Australian, Peter Rudge, published a fascinating book dealing with the organization of congregational life which he entitled, *Ministry and Management.*[1] Although Rudge is concerned primarily with the organizational structure of the Church of England, much of what he has to say has wide application. His thesis is that the way the local church organizes its common life says far more about what we believe than all that we teach and preach. It is one thing to talk about the ministry of enablement; it is quite another thing to create an organizational style that makes it possible for genuine enablement to take place. For purposes of comparison, Rudge identified five styles of congregational leadership in the church today. He is obviously pushing for his last category, the systemic model, which causes the others to be somewhat stereotyped. There is enough truth in the comparison, however, to provide a base for solid reflection. Rudge identifies his five styles of congregational life as:

1) The Traditional Model
2) The Charismatic or Intuitive Model
3) The Classical Model
4) The Human Relations Model
5) The Systemic Model

Briefly summarized, these models tend to reflect the following characteristics. In the traditional model, the primary emphasis is on the transmission of the heritage. It is essentially nonreflective and hierarchical, with a major portion of energy going toward the maintenance of the status quo. Its strength is that it provides persons with a sense of security and rootedness. Its weakness is that it cuts off new sources for vitality and growth. The traditional model does not lead toward an enabling ministry since it keeps the authority and power in the hands of the clergy.

The charismatic or intuitive model revolves around the personality of the pastor. It is prophetic, strongly rejecting the status quo, emphasizing the intuitive and spontaneous. The strength of the charismatic model rests in its vitality and flexibility. Its weakness lies in the judgmental character which tends to develop around who is *in* and who is *out*. There is also a strong tendency for heavy dependence on the leader. As in the traditional model, enablement is limited simply because "ministry" is dependent on the intuition and gifts of the charismatic leader (using charismatic to refer to one who possesses the capacity to energize others to follow his or her ideas).

The classical model tends to be hierarchical, highly rational, depending heavily on the delegation of authority and the fitting of persons into ready-made structures generally passed on over a number of years. Unlike the traditional model, the classical model might be quite innovative—indeed avant garde —but always within a highly structured environment. I remember how, in my first parish of about 150 people, we dutifully established every committee and subcommittee handed down to us by the national church. This meant, of course, that everyone had to wear numerous hats, not because it helped us get the job done but because it made us feel as if we were at the hub of things. At its best, the classical model can get a job done with efficiency and speed. Its weakness is that the *structure shapes the response* which, in turn, limits vitality and blocks interdependence. It is not a good model to facilitate enablement, largely because the emphasis is on shaping the ministries of the congregation to fit the structure, rather than having the structures that support a variety of ministries.

The human relations model is attractive because of its heavy emphasis on the personal. It is essentially nondirective, concentrating on the development of a network of intimate relationships. Heavy emphasis is placed on group development, consensus, and a high degree of personal satisfaction and commitment. The strength of the human relations model is the sense of support experienced by the membership. Its weakness lies in tending toward in-groupness and the need to maintain harmony, often at high cost. Unlike the other models, however, this way of organizing parish life does lend itself toward an enabling style, with the caveat that it also lends itself to a high degree of dependence. Genuine enablement seeks to move persons beyond dependence toward interdependence and self-initiative.

The last model in Rudge's analysis is the systemic model. The emphasis here is on interdependence and the capacity to adapt to meet changing needs. The function of the leader is not primarily to *do* ministry, but to help others identify and carry out the ministries which are uniquely theirs. The emphasis is on helping the various parts of the organization maintain sufficient connection with each other so that each part enables the other to carry out common objectives. Rudge expresses a clear preference for this model—and I think rightly so—because it provides a structure that most allows a congregation to be what it says it is. The strength of the systemic model is that it places heavy emphasis on shared authority and mutual ministry, encouraging persons to move from a posture of dependence to that of broad interdependence. Congregations sometimes find this view difficult to accept because so many of the conventions of church life militate against it. Ministers are customarily hired to "do ministry" on behalf of others. The successful pastor is not generally the one whose primary ministry is in helping others minister, but the one who is all things to all people, the stereotyped overworked parson—always loving, always available—who is not only the "leader" of the congregation but the beloved community leader as well.

III

You will note that in all of Rudge's models the pastor is at the center, which is actually the case in most congregations, regardless of one's particular doctrine of the ordained ministry. The pastor can facilitate or block the enabling process in congregational life. For good or for ill, he or she is at the focal point of the life of the congregation. The systemic approach to congregational life makes it possible for the pastor to serve as the enabler of others. Enablement has to do with the genuine sharing of gifts. It involves mutual support and accountability as everyone seeks to exercise his or her particular function of ministry. For a pastor to help bring this about (and it won't happen unless he or she is committed to at least giving it a try) there must be not only a high degree of security, but genuine skill and the ability to see things through. Despite our best efforts, the pressures against this kind of ministry are enormous.

In 1967 I was called to a church in Washington, D. C. Like many churches in the Washington area, the membership of the church included a large number of persons related to the federal government. I went to this church committed to doing all in my power to enable these persons to find workable and authentic ways to exercise their ministries in the diverse places where they found themselves. In my first year, we had a weekly breakfast meeting of state department people working on morality and foreign policy. By the end of the second year all of this had quietly disappeared. Why? No doubt there are many reasons, but one I know was a key factor. As the pressure of congregational demands began to build, I had less and less energy to give to encouraging and supporting this kind of endeavor. It was all I could do—or so it seemed—to get the help I needed to maintain a lively parish. As a result of what I see and what I have experienced, I am convinced that before there can be genuine ministry of enablement there needs to be a major attitudinal and value change—at least, for most of us. This change would give top priority to four values:

1)*It is more important for the ordained ministers in a congregation to enable others to identify and carry out their ministries than to do it themselves.* The reason for this is obvious. Each of us can do just so much, and there is normally only one ordained (which generally means seminary trained) person for numerous others who comprise the laity. The best use of the skills of the "professional" is to extend the ministry through others. This is not only theologically sound but a very practical and efficient use of the resources that are available to us.

2)*Recruiting persons for ministry is only half the task.* Without consistent and ongoing support—the hard follow-through—enablement will not take place.

3)*Interdependence is preferable to dependence.* The task of the clergy is to enable persons to move from dependence on them and what they symbolize to genuine interdependent behavior both in church and outside. This involves not only giving help to others but being able to ask help for ourselves. As Paul wrote to the church in Rome: "I want to be among you to be myself encouraged by your faith as well as you by mine" (Rom 1:12).

4)*The greatest gift a pastor has to give to another is not the right answer but the authenticity of his or her own search.* This is enabling. As Henri Nouwen has written, "When the imitation of Christ does not mean to live a life like Christ, but to live our life as authentically as Christ lived his, then there are many ways and forms in which a man can be a Christian. The minister is the one who can make this search for authenticity possible, not by standing on the side as a neutral screen or an impartial observer, but as an articulate witness of Christ, who puts his own search at the disposal of others."[2]

IV

How then do we go about the ministry of enablement in the local setting? We begin, of necessity, with our priorities. Enablement is more than an idea, it is a process that demands a particular type of vision. Once this vision is internalized, other things begin to fall into place, and functions begin to emerge, three of these are particularly crucial:

1) The Supportive Function
2) The Energizing Function
3) The Educational Function

I would like to reflect on these briefly, not to give the final word on what a pastor should or should not do in the local church but more to affirm a style of ministry, that brings into focus the many roles we are asked to fill.

First of all, *The Supportive Function.* The author of the Epistle to the Ephesians reflects on what is meant by support in the introduction to his letter, "I pray that your inward eyes may be illumined, so that you may know what is the hope to which he calls you, what the wealth and glory of the share he offers you among his people in their heritage, and how vast the resources of his power open to us who trust in him" (Eph 1:18–19). In a not dissimilar statement, Dr. Gerald Caplan of the Harvard Laboratory of Community Psychiatry defines support in this way: "An enduring pattern of continuous or intermittent ties that can be spontaneous or highly organized, but in either case serve to validate our personal identity and worth, provide genuine help with the work we are engaged in, and responds to our overall need to be dealt with as a unique individual."[3] The task of the pastor (and others as well) is to help every member of the congregation experience this kind of support. Without it, ministries will either dry up or falter.

Some of the things to consider in carrying out the supportive function would be:

1)The necessity of helping persons surface the often unrecognized "psychological contracts" that they have made with the church. This involves expectations, images of the clergy, and memories of past experiences. Helping people to get clear about their hidden contracts is a first step in enabling them to identify the kinds of ministry they might exercise.

2)A regularized system of support. The emphasis here is on a system rather than on something hit or miss. What is needed to sustain and enrich a person's ministry over the long haul? It could be a support group, a monthly luncheon with the pastor, a regular telephone call from a peer. The point is, support, to be support, must be consistent.

3)A system of accountability and recognition. If a person agrees to take a job or carry out a particular ministry, it is of crucial importance that she or he formulate and write down the things they plan to accomplish in a given time span. In this way they are establishing the norms by which they are to be held accountable, provided, of course, that those participating in the process (including the pastor) do the same thing. In this way if a job isn't done, there is a clear base on which to make changes, or if done well, to offer genuine recognition and appreciation, if only by a phone call or card.

4)Spiritual guidance and intercession. Ministry is more than a job. It is a means of expressing our own unique journeys in a particular way. The task of the enabler is to help persons

establish and maintain the kind of spiritual discipline they
need in order to be nourished by the Spirit, and to pray for
them in their vocation.

The second key function of an enabling ministry is what I call
the *Energizing Function.* We are sources of energy to others as
the creative Spirit of God is able to use us and move through
us. We energize when we make it possible for others to draw
creative energy from us—when in a very real sense we serve
as life givers. Some settings where the energizing function is
characteristically exercised are:

1)The proclamation and celebration of the story of redemption. Worship is the deepest source of energy for Christian
community. It is important, therefore, that the forms of worship be vehicles of the Spirit and not blocks that get in the way.

2)Connecting: helping parts and people to engage. Whenever
there is genuine intercommunication, there is energy. We
bring energy to a system when we are a part of that system,
aware of our impact on it, and open to feedback from it. Pastoral leadership is enabling when it helps this energizing communication to take place.

3)Caring. There are times when the greatest energy we can
bring to another person is simply to be present to them by
caring. This might involve a visit or a phone call or a meeting
—the setting is not important. What is important, however, is
the quality of what takes place between us.

4)Listening and receiving. One of the keys to the ministry of
enablement is taking the time to listen to another person "on
their turf." The best way to understand the the ministry of a
person working in an office is to engage that person in the

setting where that ministry takes place. This also seems to prevent the concerns of the local church from always being the agenda.

And finally, the *Educational Function*. Ministry is more than the exercise of good deeds. It involves being enmeshed in the Gospel story so that the great story and our own personal stories are indissolubly intertwined. Ministry involves skill and awareness. It involves a disciplined use of the resources of faith. To enable persons to discover the nature of their ministries and the resources they need to carry them out is the educational function of enablement. Four concerns seem particularly important:

1)The need to make our own journey available to others. This is at the heart of the educational enterprise, the key to genuine mutuality.

2)The need to create educational settings in which there is both trust and a spirit of exploration. It is one thing to talk about ministry, it is another to know it when we are doing it.

3)There is a need to find the kind of resources we must have to sustain ministry. Does one lawyer best nourish the ministry of another? What resources do we need? How can we best learn from one another? These are the crucial questions.

4)Enablement depends on knowing the impact of what has taken place. At the heart of the enabling process, therefore, is continuous information gathering, evaluation, and goal setting. To enable we need to know where people are. And as an enabling community, we need to be clear about where we have been and where we are going. An outside consultant can be particularly helpful in this part of the enabling process. The point is, information gathering, goal setting, and evaluation in a regular, disciplined manner are not only helpful but a major source of energy for the building up of the common life.

V

The ministry of enablement, then, is not a program but a process. It involves bringing to the surface that "full knowledge" that all of us have been given for the ministry of Jesus Christ. For genuine enablement to take place we affirm five things referred to earlier:

1)A ministry of enablement is based on a doctrine of the church which gives high priority to the development and support of the total ministry of the people of God.

2)It means the development of an organizational model which allows this theological affirmation to be expressed in practice.

3)It means an active leadership role based on support, energizing, and education.

4)It means living in the tension between active leadership and a reflective, authentic sharing of one's own journey among one's equals.

5)The ministry of enablement, like any ministry, is the work of the Spirit. We are asked only to claim who we are in Christ as authentically as we know how, for it is in this authenticity that others will find what they most need and what we have most to give.

CHAPTER VIII

Enabling the Enabler

*Adapt yourselves no longer to the
pattern of this present world, but
let your minds be remade and your
whole nature thus transformed. Then
you will be able to discern the will
of God, and to know what is good,
acceptable, and perfect.*

ROMANS 12:2

I

Not long ago I met a man who gave me a very special gift.
We were not together very long, but when our conversation
was over and we parted, I was aware of a deep thirst welling
up inside of me crying out to be quenched. I wanted to embrace all the experiences in my life that had in one way or
another caused me to grow—the books, the music, the places,
and those very special people who dot my past. I wanted to
embrace them so that they might fill me again. This man, the
gift-giver, had come to talk about retirement. At sixty-two
years of age he had served for thirty years in the ministry of
the Church. He had one concern. He wanted to plan a retirement that would allow him to follow through on the many
interests that were buried within him. The more he talked, the
more energized I became. His zest for life was more conta-
gious than I could possibly describe. His gift to me was a
lesson in the art of staying thirsty. It is a gift of which Jesus
spoke often. "I am the Alpha and the Omega," John writes of

him, "the beginning and the end. A draught from the water-springs of life will be my free gift to the thirsty" (Rev 21:6). The vitality which I sensed in my friend came from a lifelong habit of sipping at this spring.

There are many things that deepen our sense of thirst: new ideas, new relationships that demand of us genuine openness, the willingness to take risks. All of these things keep us open to new possibilities. In our most honest moments, however, we all know that thirst comes from a much deeper source. In one of the most remarkable dialogues ever recorded, Jesus, in a few moments of conversation standing by a well in Samaria introduces a woman to the mystery of her own life. "He told me everything I ever did," she recounts later. What Jesus did was to point her inward to the source of spiritual energy that up to this point had never fully been tapped, energy which Jesus compares with an inner spring constantly welling up within us.

Genuine thirst, the thirst that keeps us alive and growing, emerges from the tension between the cultivation of our inner journey and our response to the world around us. Authentic ministry emerges out of the creative balance between these two poles. James Wall, the editor of *Christian Century*, suggests that all of us seem to have two quite strong but opposing characteristics: we are both artist and politician.[1] The artist creates; the politician negotiates. The artist dreams dreams; the politician solves problems. The artist explores the new land, beholding in awe the beauty of the trees. The politician settles the land, cutting down the trees for fire and shelter. When these two aspects of life are held in tension there is a vitality and thirst. When the tension slacks, we are left either in a world of fantasy or a world of manipulation. Each world, by itself, is ultimately empty and superficial.

Each of us, of course, is different in our approach to minis-try. We seek to maintain balance in our lives in a number of different ways. I suspect that for most of us, however, it is easier to affirm the politician than the artist. The pressures of institutional life have a way of subduing the artist. There seems never to be enough time to dream or to explore or to make friends with solitude. At the heart of the enabling ministry, then, lies this sense of balance. There are jobs to be done, jobs of critical importance, but unless there is the cultivation of that deeper awareness from which genuine authenticity comes, there will be no real mutuality between those who share the ministry of the people of God. Enabling those that enable others is the task of the whole church. It involves a commitment to nurturing the thirst from which growth comes.

One of the major underlying themes of this book is that the local congregation has a primary responsibility to enable persons to discover and exercise the ministries they have been given. In the chapters preceding this one, I have sought to point out what some of these ministries might look like and how a church might set about the enabling process. This brings us to a critical fact about congregational life. The pastor, for good or for ill, is in a position to encourage and support or to block and dilute whatever initiative emerges in the congregation at large. When he or she is inept or depressed, the life of the entire congregation is affected. When he or she is excited about what is going on, and is growing inwardly and acquiring new skills, the congregation is generally the primary beneficiary.

The issue of lay education is of critical importance to the vitality of the local church and the integrity of its mission to the world. The continuing education and professional development of the clergy is of equal importance to the church, simply because it is so intimately related. The plain fact is, you cannot have one without the other. Both are of concern to the local congregation.

The issue, however, is not as simple as it may seem. Enabling the enabler requires more than a pastor taking a course here or a workshop there. In order to improve the quality of their enabling ministry, we need to look at the entire system by which pastors are encouraged and supported in pursuing their own professional development. An effective program of continuing education must be a long-range process in which clergy, in consultation with others, make choices for themselves that expand their competence, keep their creative juices flowing, and deepen their sense of vocation. Unless a program is long-range, it is not continuing; and unless it is freely chosen and involves the whole person (including his or her faith commitment), it is not education in the best sense of the word.

II

It is the purpose of this chapter to provide a resource for clergy and congregational and denominational leaders to think through what is needed on an ongoing basis to sustain a genuinely enabling ministry. For starters I have identified six issues that need to be considered. They are not intended to be exhaustive, but rather they are extensions of some of the themes that have been developed throughout this book.

Personal Renewal

The ordained ministry is often a life of intense intimacy and intense loneliness. The moments of intimacy come in many ways: sharing another person's pain, preparing a couple for marriage, or through those moments of deep silence found in prayer either by one's self or in the company of others. Since these moments, however, are generally not sustained, they are always followed by feelings of bereavement. The feeling of loneliness can be most intense when one is surrounded by people. When it comes, it generally opens the door to companion feelings of disappointment, dryness, and fatigue. There is so much to be done, so many legitimate demands to be met, so much stimuli that, when the door is open, feelings flood in that can be overwhelming. In times like these, avenues to personal and spiritual renewal need to be opened. While the need varies from person to person and from situation to situation, one factor seems to be present whatever the setting: it is hardest to ask for help when we most need it.

At the heart of enabling the enabler lies the need for continuous spiritual renewal and theological stimulation. There is no substitute for this. Without it we begin to dry up inside. A congregation needs to provide time and money for such renewal and, even more important, ecouragement. Only when we are renewed by the power of the Spirit within, are we able to be sources of renewal to others.

The effectiveness of any long-range program of continuing education lies in the balance it is able to achieve between content and skill (realizing that there is content involved in developing skill, and skill involved in mastering content). With sabbatical leaves becoming common in the church, more ministers have the opportunity to go back to a seminary or university for a semester to explore a particular subject area or to build a sabbatical program around a series of short-term experiences focused on a particular theme. In consulting with persons planning a sabbatical I have found it helpful to have them write out their expectations for their time away, out of which learning goals can be developed. In this way it is easier to determine what the sabbatical will involve and why. In a situation where a person is putting together study leave by connecting a series of short-term events offered by a number of institutions, it is also helpful to keep a journal throughout the experience so that a summary paper can be written at the conclusion of the time. This not only helps with motivation and clarity, it also enables people to generalize about their study theme in a way that has long-range possibilities.

In addition to the ever-present need for personal renewal, which includes the ability to ask hard questions of ourselves, there are also specific skills required for the kind of enabling ministry needed by the congregation. Although, in some sense they may seem obvious, they are noted here because they are normally not included in a pastor's seminary training. It is assumed that a pastor has these skills, when the plain fact is that, unless there has been a special effort made to develop them, these skills are present only to the degree that they have been learned by experience or possessed by instinct. What is needed, however, is more than this. We need pastors who have mastered the art of the enabling process. The following skills are fundamental to this process and can be learned:

1.Skills in group development—including the ability to handle conflict creatively and to give and receive constructive criticism.

2.The ability to guide others in their spiritual journey—the art of spiritual direction.

3.Caring, consultation, and support skills—disciplines that are now highly developed in many of the helping professions.

4.Skills in communication—the ability to frame clear questions, to listen, and to articulate ideas in a way that communicates feeling as well as content.

This list does not pretend to be exhaustive. Immediately such things as educational skills and management skills come to mind and, of course, are extremely important. The above, however, are fundamental to the enabling process. While no skill can be a substitute for a life informed and shaped by the power of Christ, the development of our skills is one way we have to be responsible for the gifts we have been given.

The second issue we need to address is that of increasing the stake of the congregation in the ongoing education of their clergy. Continuing education is not only a concern of clergy and church officials, but of the congregation as well. Clergy need to sit down with appropriate groups in their congregations to plan for their developmental needs. Until this happens, there is no way for congregations to see the development of the clergy as a concern in which they have a vital part. With coordinated planning, cooperative funding could be more effectively worked out between the clergy, the congregation, the denomination, and the seminary (or whatever other institution is involved). This kind of cooperative funding does not now exist, but the need is acute.

In a 1974 Hartford Seminary Foundation survey of continuing education goals of clergy, two major obstacles were noted: time and money.[2] Aside from the need for cooperation in matters of funding noted above, there is a much deeper issue involved. Congregations need to understand that investment in the continuing education of their pastor is an investment in the vitality of their corporate life. In most parishes, the salary of the clergy person is the largest single item in the budget. Funds budgeted for continuing education, therefore—based on a realistic assessment of the actual costs of ongoing education—constitute protection of a major investment already made by the congregation.

The issue of time, although relatively simple at first glance, seems to involve a number of complex subtleties. Many congregations are jealous of their pastor's time and simply resent the time when he or she is away. Some lay persons tend to see study leave as vacation. Because of these misunderstandings, an ongoing educational process within the congregation is necessary. Opportunities need to be provided for members of the congregation to react to the learning goals established by the pastor and, at the end of a particular program, to hear the results.

An even more subtle factor, however, is the resistance of the clergy person to time off. Zealousness of this kind, with all the illusion of indispensibility that comes with it, often stems from deep feelings of insecurity and inadequacy which need to be responded to with care. This condition is a symptom of the absence of mutuality. Most parish clergy work six days a week plus two or three nights a week. On any comparative scale, this is a heavy time demand which puts intense pressure on family life and, I am convinced, has an increasingly debilitating effect on both morale and creativity. In the last parish I served, I was given one weekend off every two months in addition to a month's vacation and two week's study leave which I could take throughout the year. Since my wife was employed and my children were in school, my church felt we needed time to be together throughout the year. For me personally, it meant a sense of being relieved from what, when I was tired, felt all too much like routine. I found that I didn't use all of the weekends, but it was tremendously freeing to know I could. It is interesting that every time I have suggested this to another congregation or pastor, the immediate response, made either defensively or else hopelessly, is to recite all the reasons why such an idea would not work. Maybe not, but the issue of time and ongoing growth continues to be a serious one.

Self-Assessment

The third issue has to do with the relationship of continuing education to professional self-assessment. If continuing education is indeed to increase one's competency and sense of self-worth, what the minister does in continuing education needs to be related to those areas of ministry where he feels most need as well as to those areas which are part of his "growing edge." As a result of all the work now being done with methods of professional assessment for clergy, we are beginning to learn some things that are terribly important. There is no doubt that if ongoing assessment is to increase motivation for growth rather than deter it, its use must rest primarily in the hands of those who are being assessed. Professional assessment or performance evaluation is a resource for growth used voluntarily by those people who see it as a resource and not as a threat. To be effective it should involve the person seeking information on his or her ministry, members of the congregation who are involved in this ministry, and selected colleagues with whom he or she works.

The primary aim of professional assessment, whatever the method used, is to identify areas for ongoing development. The need, therefore, is to develop strategies and models for the disciplined assessment of one's ministry that is perceived as a resource and not a threat, and that is tied to our ongoing need for continued education. Until we do this more effectively, we are going to continue to plan too many programs not on the basis of genuine need but in terms of current fads. It could well be that if a pastor could be helped to see that if his or her preaching generally improved, his or her sense of satisfaction might be far greater than the benefits received from a three-day workshop on Transactional Analysis. With genuine and consistent feedback and support, it is possible to plan for needs on a more realistic basis. To begin thinking this way is going to require real discipline, but it seems to me to be at the heart of the problem.

One pastor in a middle-sized New England congregation began planning for his continuing education on the basis of needs in the congregation that he was not meeting. With the help of his ministry development committee, interviews were conducted in the congregation to determine where people were feeling most need of support from the pastor. Several areas emerged including a deep concern on the part of many persons for real direction in the area of prayer and spiritual growth. On the basis of this assessment, the pastor worked out a three-year plan aimed at deepening both his own gifts and strengthening his ability to serve as a spiritual guide to others. The plan was adjusted several times but it served nevertheless to relate a genuine concern for personal growth with the ongoing need for competency in ministry.

Developmental Programming

The fourth issue concerns what might be called the need for developmental programming, an issue closely related to that of self-assessment. Continuing education offerings need to be seen both in the context of self-initiated, long-term learning goals and in relation to the rhythms we seem to experience as growing adults. One function of a denominational continuing education committee might be to provide assistance to clergy in planning long-term programs for their own professional development. In some cases this would involve a series of short-term experiences over a two- or three-year period; in others, a study term in a seminary or pastoral training center pursuing specific subject matter. This would mean that one task of the continuing education committee would be to know enough about the developmental plans of the persons with whom it was working so as to be able to respond to genuine need either as a jurisdiction or as a broker to other institutions.

In the studies of continuing education, the greatest need expressed was for a disciplined program of study that was developmental in nature and in short enough time sequences to be feasible for the working pastor.[3] The Doctor of Ministry programs is one attempt to respond to this need. The question it raises, however, is what happens after the D.Min. has been awarded? Does professional development cease, or does the process of getting the D.Min. have built into it the seeds of ongoing development? One response is to avoid the D.Min. route altogether, concentrating on more short-term programs which make use of the Continuing Education Unit (one unit for ten hours of work) as a method of measurement. The key, of course, is flexibility, to encourage persons by whatever means possible to pursue goals that are rewarding to themselves.

No one is going to be intensively involved in programs of continuing education all the time. We seem to move from periods of intense involvement to plateaus of assimilation and practice. Events occur in our lives, however, that disrupt these rhythms: a move from one church to another, a bad adjustment to the much written about mid-career crisis, early fears about one's retirement, a personal emotional crisis—any of these very common experiences could well disrupt the rhythm of growth and assimilation. What kind of interventions are most useful either in getting the rhythm going again or starting for the first time? Does the minister always have to ask for help or are there other kinds of initiatives which are both supportive and effective? This is an issue which very much needs to be addressed, not only for the sake of the minister himself but for the sake of genuine mutuality in the enabling ministry.

Overcoming Fear

The fifth issue might well be the most difficult and the most serious issue those concerned with continuing education must face. It is related to the breakdown of the growth and assimilation rhythm referred to previously, but it goes much deeper. The issue of which I speak is one of apathy and fear. The more alone and inadequate one feels, the greater is the threat of exposure. I shall never forget as a young priest just beginning my ministry being told by an older man who I looked up to and respected how uneasy he felt around me and my peers.

"The plain fact is," he said, "I feel out of date and out of touch." In the last fifteen years of ministry this man did nothing to either update himself or "get back in touch," not because the need was not there but because the fear was stronger than the need.

Most clergy who serve in the local church very early in their ministries develop what I would best describe as a "loner" method of operation. You learn to do your own thing as effectively as possible with a minimum of help from anyone else. To ask help from one's peers is somehow viewed as lack of competence. As a result, when we get together with our colleagues, especially those we don't know too well, it is far easier to express what we feel most negative about either in the Church or in the world around us, than to expose those areas of ministry where we feel genuinely vulnerable. The issue of which we speak is obviously a very complex one. There is much in every denomination which encourages this kind of guardedness and isolation, but if we are concerned with the question of motivation, the issue of apathy related to fear is very real indeed.

Coordination

Finally, issue number six. It is my conviction that continuing education within the Church faces us with a systemic problem of massive proportions. We simply cannot separate our concern for ongoing education from such things as personal satisfaction, ongoing self-assessment, our ability to influence the system of which we are a part, pastoral care, ongoing support, and such mundane things as job placement and salary. Nor can we separate the work of the ministry from the deeper things which give meaning and substance to our vocation: spiritual growth, continuous encounter with the Scriptures, opportunities to reformulate our theological understanding in the light of new experience. All are integrally related. The question before us is: "What has to happen to bring about the kind of coordination we so desperately need?" We need to learn how to use what we have in ways that avoid duplication, in a context that takes the many facets of ministry with genuine seriousness. It has been demonstrated time and time again that clergy will respond to those things that are clearly going to affect their sense of well-being and self-worth.

III

When we speak then of continuing education in the Church, we are speaking of a many-faceted process that goes on from ordination *through* retirement (and I use "through" intentionally, since retirement hardly brings an end to the need to grow). To be effective, the initiative for ongoing development must be in the hands of the person involved. The congregation can encourage this process in a number of ways; serving where needed as evaluator, supporter, and facilitator. There are obviously times when direct intervention is needed. For some of the reasons we have noted, many clergy need help in taking responsibility for their ongoing development. Much of this help can come from the congregation, but some responsibility needs to be exercised by the denomination. It is my dream that the time will soon come when the local church, the denomination judicatory, the seminary, or other continuing education agencies will not only share information in a disciplined way but will plan and program together to achieve the maximum possible impact. There is no better way to model what we believe than to begin with ourselves. Ministry involves serving as enablers to one another.

The local church gathers together persons of diverse gifts to celebrate the life-giving presence of God in the world, to rehearse that story that gives them identity, and then to disperse to carry out the ministry of Christ to the world. The function of the ordained person in this community is to represent through that office the symbolic presence that makes this community different from other associations in which people gather; and, as a fellow pilgrim, to enable others to discover and use their gifts to the glory of God. These concerns are everyone's concerns; simply because they are basic to what it means to be the Church. Ongoing growth, the art of staying thirsty, is not an option for Christian ministry; it is at the heart of our life in Christ.

CHAPTER IX

A Vision of the Church-to-Be

*Then he who sat on the throne said, "Behold! I
am making all things new!" (And he said to me,
"Write this down; for these words are trustworthy
and true. Indeed they are already fulfilled.") I am
the Alpha and the Omega, the beginning and the end.*

REVELATION 21:5–6

I

Since the beginning of time the religious impulse has produced in men and women the capacity to dream dreams of
the future. This envisioning process is a necessary element in
any kind of creative planning. Ezekiel envisioned a valley of
dry bones given new life by the breath of God. St. John envisioned the new age which God would bring into being out of
the remnant of a persecuted church. When anchored in reality, visions of the future can be a source both of necessary
judgment and creative energy. The old visions that at one
time gave shape to the world's imagination have lost their
power. It is time for a new vision to emerge, a vision shaped
not by the technology of man, but by the redemptive power
of God.

There is no way to look at the world of tomorrow without
coming face-to-face with the most significant social fact of our
time: the separation of the values inherent in increased production from the values concerned with human survival. A
life-style based on consumption, and that disregards the larger

issue of what it means to be human, contains the seeds of its own destruction. This issue, with all its vast ramifications, is at the heart of the convulsive changes we are just beginning to experience.

We cannot begin to envision the church of the future without taking seriously the kind of world in which we as the church will exist. "The civilizational malaise, in a word," writes Robert Heilbroner, "reflects the inability of a civilization directed toward material improvement—higher incomes, better diets, miracles of medicine, triumphs of applied physics and chemistry—to satisfy the human spirit. There is," he notes later, "nowhere to turn other than to those private beliefs and disbeliefs that guide each of us through life, and whose disconcerting presence was the foremost problem with which we had to deal in appraising the prospect before us."[1]

We are indeed on the threshold of a new age. As the church looks to the future, it will have to confront five forces that will play a major role in shaping the world that is emerging. They are:

1. A reordering of priorities brought about by a decrease in resources.

2. The anxiety produced by the fact of change.

3. A demand for more equitable participation in the human community.

4. An increased thirst for spiritual experience.

5. The quest for simplicity.

II

First of all, any vision of the future of the local church needs to be seen in the context of those strong pressures that are forcing a reordering of priorities. The most obvious pressures are economic. As costs increase and resources become more limited, we are already being forced to make some hard choices about buildings and budgets. We are going to see a continued decline in funds available for special ministries; churches with multiple staffs may be required to cut back, increasing the problem of clergy placement but giving encouragement to efforts for greater mobilization of the laity. It may well be that we are approaching the age of the laity in a way unparalleled since the first centuries of the church. How we mobilize to respond to this reality will be of critical importance to what has historically been (even in the so-called free churches) a clerically dominated church.

Probably the most difficult issue to face, however, will be the economic feasibility of the time-honored tradition of each congregation owning its own building solely for its own purposes. If we are to maintain our presence in areas where we can no longer be self-supporting, we will need to ask ourselves with far greater seriousness than we have done in the past: "Are there alternative ways to sustain the community of faith?" "Is it not possible to sell our property and rent space in a building not being used at times most needed by the church—evenings and Sundays?" "And if we begin doing this, how do we re-educate the community of faith to look for the church in places other than in the white-steepled building on the green?" These are the critical questions. Suburban churches that have begun in schools or in other buildings have almost always moved rapidly to build their own buildings. In most cases, after the initial organizing period, growth did not noticably take place until the building was occupied. People identify church with a "church building."

There are other alternatives. Some churches have quite deliberately sought to rent out space to others. Others have turned to mergers or the increased use of part-time clergy. In some areas coalitions have developed in which the resources of the more affluent churches have been shared with congregations less well-off. Whatever the nature of the response, however, we are being forced to ask a very fundamental question: "What is it we *really* need in order to call ourselves a Christian congregation?"

A large suburban congregation in North Carolina just recently faced this question as a matter of values before it became a matter of budget. In the midst of a major capital funds drive for a new addition to already expansive physical facilities, the decision was made not to build more but to use the funds toward a disciplined response to the problem of world hunger. Although for most congregations such dramatic action might not be feasible, the issue remains the same: "What indeed are the priorities we must affirm to remain faithful to the Gospel in a world of scarcity?"

III

The problem of priority is not solely a matter of buildings and budget. It involves even more fundamentally what we understand to be basic to the Christian faith. This question is doubly important in a time when anxiety is especially high. If all the predictions are accurate, the pace and convulsive nature of change are rapidly increasing, and will continue to increase. It is inevitable, therefore, that anxiety over both the instability of the present and uncertainty over the future will increase also. How then can we find a faith that will provide a sense of certainty in a time when there is so little to be certain about? The way we as the church respond to this question is of critical importance for the future.

On the positive side we are being pushed to reaffirm with increased conviction that we are indeed bearers of good news. We have a story to tell—a Gospel to proclaim—that gives meaning to human existence. There are signs that we are once again beginning to take our evangelistic heritage seriously. We are beginning to reaffirm what it means to have a ministry that involves sharing the good news with someone else. The time of timidity is over. We have a story to tell and there is an urgency about telling it. The congregation which acts on this reality is a congregation in touch with tomorrow.

In any return to so-called fundamentals there is a terrible temptation to settle for easy answers. When faced with the anxiety of turmoil there is always strong pressure to grasp for a faith that is more and more exclusive and less and less tolerant of ambiguity. This does have the effect of minimizing the threat, but at the risk of distorting the meaning of the Gospel. There are countless numbers of people, and there will be countless more, who are struggling to find a faith that will give meaning and purpose to human existence in a way that keeps them open to the great questions facing the world. The deeper answer to anxiety does not lie in increased certainty, but in the courage to live creatively in the midst of ambiguity and paradox. This is what faith is about.

"The function of faith," writes Thomas Merton, "is not to reduce mystery to rational clarity, but to integrate the unknown and the known together in a living whole, in which we are more and more able to transcend the limitation of our external self. . . . True faith is never merely a source of spiritual comfort," he continues. "It may indeed bring peace, but before it does so it must involve us in struggle."[2] Faith comes as we find a center for our lives that stands beyond the ebb and flow of human events but is always related to them. Jesus Christ is that center. It is the conviction and experience of the community of faith that as we open our lives to him at ever-deepening levels of our existence, we will not only be able to cope with the anxiety that surrounds us but, more important still, have a gift of profound importance to offer to others.

The church of the future will be a church deeply involved in the rediscovery of its biblical heritage. It is in the engagement with Scripture that we are called into the great questions of human existence, not to find answers which close us off but to live into these questions as through the Spirit the answers unfold. "All the evidence of human experience," writes Leslie Newbegin, "the evidence of the greatest of men, the poets, the artists, the scientists and the saints, goes to suggest that knowledge is accessible to those who are ready to keep the door open to venture beyond what is clear and unquestionable, even if it involves the risk of being mistaken or talking nonsense. . . . The active principle is the willingness to go out beyond what is certain, to listen to what is not yet clear, to search for what is hardly visible, to venture the affirmation which may prove to be wrong, but which may also prove to be the starting point for new conquests of the mind. In the traditional language of Christianity the name for that active principle is faith."[3]

IV

The third major force strongly present in society, and therefore confronting the church, is the increasing demand by more and more people for more equitable participation in the human community. On the national scene we see this demand by black Americans, Indian Americans, Hispanic Americans, women's groups, and other groups who for one reason or another feel themselves to be oppressed. These movements are reflections of even greater forces bursting forth all over the world. The day of the "have nots" is fast emerging, and, for the sake of the wholeness of the human community, the church must respond to this new condition. When we speak of the demands of this group or that group for more equal participation in the human community, we are talking about the very nature of community itself. The issue is not whether a particular congregation agrees with the aims of the Gay Liberation Movement, but rather how, while maintaining its own convictions, it can build a bridge to that part of itself which is the Gay Movement—or the Women's Movement or the Black Movement. The issue is one of community and this is the church's business.

Dean Colin Williams of the Yale Divinity School speaks of the need for what he calls, "the three-story church."[4] The second story, or the main floor of the church, is the body of the congregation who look to the church for stimulation and support. By and large they are more receivers than givers. The third or upper story is the parish apostolate, those groups of laity who have taken on with the pastor a genuinely mutual ministry. These groups, or task forces of committed and disciplined people, are organized to respond to particular needs both within and without the congregation. The first floor, or basement, is made up of those groups who do not fit the conventional mode, yet are still members or potential participants in the church's life: counterculture groups, political radicals, or what have you. Williams puts them on the basement floor to indicate the need for ongoing dialogue between basement groups and first-story groups. Community takes place when personhood is affirmed. The church in recent years has had difficulty with diversity, and yet diversity is our heritage. "Parthians, Medes, Elamites . . . Jews and proselytes, Cretans and Arabs, we hear them telling in our own tongues the great things God has done" (Acts 2:9–11).

Any vision of the future that is faithful to the Gospel of Christ places the church squarely and unequivocally on the side of the poor and downtrodden. "The Spirit of the Lord is upon me," proclaimed Jesus as he began his ministry, "because he has annointed me; he has sent me to announce good news to the poor, to proclaim release for prisoners and recovery of sight for the blind, to let the broken victims go free, to proclaim the year of the Lord's favour" (Lk 4:18,19).

Since the era of Constantine, the Christian Church identified with the parts of the social system that are in control,
whatever these might be. For all intents and purposes, the
churches of America are indeed part of the establishment. If
we are to criticize those values and institutions in our society
that dehumanize and destroy, we must recognize with humility that we are part of these very same values and institutions.
This being the case, it is of critical importance that the church
of the West develop strategies that will continually hold up at
the local level the plight of the poor and the hungry and the
politically dispossessed, both the world over and in our own
backyards. Such strategies will undoubtedly create conflict
and anger. This is the price we must pay if we are to grasp the
future that is upon us. Problems of hunger, unemployment,
welfare, and vast differences in income are fundamental to the
Gospel. The integrity of our response to this issue alone might
be the most serious challenge we face. Douglas Hall has written that the only way the Western church can be healed of its
blindness is through total "disestablishment" from the culture
of affluence. "What might it mean," he writes, ". . . if in our
time the Christian churches of North America began to say
and do things radically different from the dominant culture?
What if it happened that people all over the globe began to
learn that within North America, a people existed who chose
to resist the way of affluence and power in the name of Jesus
Christ."[5]

Questions like these, questions now being echoed throughout the third world, must be faced squarely on the local as well
as the national scene. Whatever strategies we adopt must be
hammered out against a backdrop of these prophetic voices of
world liberation that are now calling us to account. As we are
faithful in this task, we will discover, as the church has discov-

ered in the past, what the Lord means by his promise to "make all things new."

V

The fourth major force confronting society, and particularly the church, is the inward search for authentic spiritual experience. We see this search manifested in the United States in three rather distinct ways. The first of these is the rapidly expanding series of secular and humanistic approaches such as Transcendental Meditation and Transpersonal Psychology. Secondly, it is probably safe to say that the major religions of the East are sufficiently established in this country to be a permanent addition to our religious heritage. This is especially true of the more popular and mystical expressions of Eastern religion such as Zen, Sufiism, and Yoga. Finally, we are beginning to see a serious effort to recover the contemplative tradition in Christianity, an effort which, from the church's point of view, needs to be supported and encouraged.

Not long ago I was in a plane on my way home from a meeting in North Carolina. I was reading Jacob Needleman and Dennis Lewis's book, *Sacred Tradition and Present Need*, which caught the attention of the man sitting next to me and which ultimately led to a fascinating conversation. He was an international salesman for the General Electric Corporation, who a year previously had spiritually and emotionally almost reached the end of his rope. The time away from home and the pressure of his job had disrupted both his family life and his own interior sense of self. Through a colleague at work he was introduced to Transcendental Meditation and on his own (with only a book for a guide) began the practice of meditation. The experience awakened in him a longing for this element in his own tradition (he was Roman Catholic) and he went to his church seeking help. For one reason or another, he was turned away, or at least, he felt turned away. The result has been that his meditative life has become more and more cut off from its roots. "Everywhere I go," he said, "I meet meditators. I was in Cincinnati the other day and happened to mention to the plant manager my interest in TM only to find out he too was a meditator. As a matter of fact, he called in one of his cohorts who was a meditator also and we spent the next hour sharing our experiences."

This conversation, more than anything else I have encountered, made me realize the intensity of the quest for spiritual experience now being expressed in this country. It has made me ask: "Why the attraction to the contemplative disciplines?" I am convinced that one answer lies in our saturation with words. In a mass media culture such as our own, we are literally engulfed in words to the point that, for many people, words have begun to lose their power. I worry about the readiness of the church to jump too quickly to an evangelistic style which depends so heavily on the spoken word ("Brother, do you love Jesus?"). For if the church is to take seriously what seems to be happening, it needs to develop an environment in which people are encouraged to talk less and listen more.

John Biersdorf, Director of the Institute for Advanced Pastoral Studies, has made the very interesting observation that "the appeal of non-Western religions in this culture is due largely to their ability to furnish practical disciplines and methods for attaining enlightenment. We have rightly emphasized our conviction that we are ultimately only justified by faith. This emphasis, however," he continues, "combined with the separation of spiritual disciplines from other methods of personal fulfillment by secular psychology has tended to cut off Christian groups even from the historic disciplines of their own tradition."[6]

If we are to take these comments seriously, as I believe we

must, it is essential that we intensify the dialogue between Christianity and others concerned with the inner quest. It has taken years to recover from the antagonistic position which the church took in the early days of the psychological revolution pioneered by Sigmund Freud. It would be a tragedy if this kind of separation took place again. The church has much to learn from both Transpersonal Psychology and the great traditions of the East. We have much to learn also in the recovery of our own contemplative heritage. Both of these are critical as we approach the future that is fast upon us.

VI

The final movement which I have noted concerns what seems best described as the quest for simplicity. It began in the tumultuous days of the 60s on a sensational plane with the "Hippies" and the "Flower Children," but more seriously with those many diverse groups who sought to create and sustain an alternative to the life-style which typified middle-class America. Many of the values once limited to the counter-culture are now making their way into the thinking of vast numbers of persons throughout the nation. Economic scarcity is forcing upon us an increasing unease about our uncritical consumer orientation. There is genuine concern on the part of more and more people over the rapidly multiplying imbalance that exists in the world—an imbalance that places this nation, which consumes forty-four percent of the world's resources, squarely in the center of the problem.

The expression of this concern takes many forms. For some families it has meant a disciplined reduction of food consumption; for others, a self-conscious attempt to break the dependency upon the automobile. For still others, this sense of unease cuts even more deeply. As one stockbroker expressed it in a very honest moment, "I sometimes wonder if the competitiveness and demand for increased profits on which our system depends is not carrying us to our own destruction. I don't have the answers. I only know it's beginning to concern me more and more."

The quest for simplicity is no longer the exclusive property of the counterculture, if it ever was. For increasing numbers of people, life-styles geared to affluence and abundance are open to serious question. For many, such a life-style is in direct contradiction to those values inherent in the Christian Gospel. If the church is to be faithful to the Gospel mandate, we are called to be in the vanguard of the quest for a more equitable life style. No question we face has any greater ethical implications.

The quest for a more simplified life-style, however, can be easily romanticized. For persons long accustomed to the accepted "American standard of living," change is not as easy as it seems. One family reported the difficulties they encountered trying to move to a smaller house. They lived in a large old house which they had obtained at a bargain price several years previously at a low mortgage rate. The rise of fuel costs, however, forced them to consider not only the expense of maintaining the house, but the disproportionate amount of energy they were consuming when viewed in the context of world energy needs. After much discussion, they decided to sell, only to discover it would cost them more to move to a smaller house than to stay where they were. The increase in mortgage rates, the increase in housing costs, and the cost of the move itself confronted them squarely with the systemic implications of their decision. They discovered, as have many others, that the decision to alter one aspect of one's life touches many others as well.

The way we live is a concrete expression of the values we hold. What we buy, what we possess, the decisions we make with regard to our environment, not only deeply affect us inwardly but will have far-reaching effects on the lives of others with whom we share the planet as well as to those who come after us. Simple living is not a single issue, but it is, nevertheless, an issue about which we can make some clear decisions and take definitive action.

A very fine publication entitled *Taking Charge* offers a number of very practical ways that Christians can go about simplifying their style of life. The secret rests in our willingness, as the title of the book suggests, to take charge. "Taking charge," the author writes, "means taking conscious responsibility for the decisions we make every day in relation to our use of resources, energy and food. The decisions are too often, we submit, either made automatically or taken for granted. . . . Simple living is a many-faceted process. It embodies personal and communal growth and development as commitment to political and social change. We wish, in George Lackey's words, to bring the future into the present—both in our own lives and in the environment in which we live."[7]

If the congregation is to be in touch with the future, it must find ways in its own institutional life to bear witness to the simplicity of the Gospel, while at the same time giving support and encouragement to those who are trying to live more simply. One very practical step was developed by a group in Philadelphia. Known as the Shakertown Pledge, it is an attempt to provide a way for people to act on the basis of values that contribute to a more simple and intentional life. The nine points of the pledge are stated as follows:

> Recognizing that the earth and the fulness thereof is a gift from our gracious God, and that we are called to cherish, nurture, and provide loving stewardship for the earth's resources,
>
> And recognizing that life itself is a gift, and a call to responsibility, joy, and celebration,

I make the following declarations:

1. I declare myself to be a world citizen.
2. I commit myself to lead an ecologically sound life.
3. I commit myself to lead a life of creative simplicity and to share my personal wealth with the world's poor.
4. I commit myself to join with others in reshaping institutions in order to bring about a more just global society in which each person has full access to the needed resources for her/his physical, emotional, intellectual, and spiritual growth.
5. I commit myself to occupational accountability, and in so doing I will seek to avoid the creation of products which cause harm to others.
6. I affirm the gift of my body, and commit myself to its proper nourishment and physical well-being.
7. I commit myself to examine continually my relations with others, and to attempt to relate honestly, morally, and lovingly to those around me.
8. I commit myself to personal renewal through prayer, meditation, and study.
9. I commit myself to responsible participation in a community of faith.

VII

I have always found it helpful in the early stages of any planning process to let my mind dream about what it would be like if nothing stood in the way of my doing the most exciting and creative things I could think of. In planning for the future of a congregation it would mean that you could dream what it would be like if: there were no customs to follow, there were no financial restraints, people all agreed with your ideas, you could have any kind of organization you wanted, and so on. This aspect of planning is generally referred to as "envisioning." By taking away restraints it allows our creative juices to flow, ideas and new possibilities to surface that would not normally emerge. When everyone involved has had a chance to do this, common themes can be noted and we can ask the practical questions: "Which of these seems to make sense for us?" "What would prevent us from doing this or that?" When there is some agreement on what the new possibilities might be, they can be built into a plan for the future.

One vision of a congregation might look like this. The congregation is gathered for carefully planned worship. About two hundred people are present: men, women, children, old people, and young people of a variety of races and circumstances. The service is a good blend of solemnity and spontaneity involving a number of people in the congregation. The Scripture is read with great care, and then people are invited into silence and a brief moment of sharing with a person nearby. The service is led by three people. The preacher is an ordained woman who is employed full-time as chief pastor of the congregation. Presiding at the Eucharist is an ordained man who works part-time in the church and part-time as a social worker in the community. Intercessions are led by an insurance salesman currently serving as president of the congregation. It is the custom in this congregation for the lay president to receive a small stipend for the considerable time he is asked to give.

The church building is old and historic. The parish hall, however, is new, containing offices rented to various groups in the community. Since commitment is high in the congregation, the financial support of the congregation is high as well. With minimal expenses it allows fifty percent of the income to be placed in an Advocacy Fund to support concerns and projects and people voted on by the congregation.

To become a member of the congregation it is necessary to participate in a year-long orientation program. Its aim is to help people to get a sense of the movement of their own story as it relates to the story of faith and to help them identify the kind of ministry that they would like to undertake. It should be noted that as soon as a new family or individual comes to the church they are visited by two persons who not only share something about the church (and themselves) but who help the new people get clear about what they want from a church, including what they expect from the pastor. In this way a covenant is developed based on clear expectations.

The congregation is made up of a number of ministry groups, some of which meet regularly at the church, others of which meet in the city. Several of these groups have adopted a common spiritual discipline including a commitment to a simplified life-style. These ministry groups, seven in number, are focused on a number of concerns ranging from caring for members of the church who are sick or in difficulty to projects in the community. One such group is made up mostly of high-school age young people whose ministry involves helping other young people find jobs. All of the ministry groups participate in a training program concerned with evangelism in contemporary society.

The involvement of those not in ministry groups (and these continually change) takes place on Sunday morning both in worship and in the Sunday educational process, which involves both adults and children, sometimes separate and sometimes together. Everyone is also invited to the monthly parish meeting where much of the community's business is transmitted, where there is a common meal, followed by some specific program ranging from a debate to a parish square dance. And so it goes.

All of us are rightly concerned with the future. The vision described above is only one of many possibilities. The point is, when we wrestle with declining church budgets and sparsely filled churches, as many of us do, it is very easy to lose sight of that vision in which new possibilities reside. Visions are expressions of our faith.

As Christians we dare to affirm that God's creation of the world continues. We dare to affirm that within us and around us everything is being shaped and reshaped by loving hands. The life of Jesus of Nazareth continues to impact even the darkest corners of human experience. For countless millions of people the point of this impact has been and will continue to be the local church. Martin Marty writes: "Sometimes theologians are naïve about social science and especially about history. They act as if 'once upon a time' there were parishes that were perfectly organized to fulfill God's purposes and that only today they are failing. I know a magazine which has a standard answer when people write in and say, 'Your magazine is not as good as it used to be.' The editors write an answer, 'You are right. It never was.' So with the parish. It never was 'as good as it used to be.'"[7]

As long as there are Christians there will be communities of faith—congregations of people gathered for worship and witness in the cities, towns, and crossroads of the world. The question is not *if* but *how*—the question that, by the grace of God, turns us in hope to the future, which is now.

Notes

INTRODUCTION

1. Walker Percy, *The Moviegoer*. Popular Library, New York, 1962, p. 17.

Chapter I

1. Robert L. Heilbroner, *An Inquiry into the Human Prospect*. W. W. Norton, New York, 1974. p. 132.

2. Douglas John Hall, *The Reality of the Gospel and the Unreality of the Churches*. Westminster, Philadelphia, 1975. p. 97.

3. Thomas Merton, *New Seeds of Contemplation*. New Directions, New York, 1961. p. 32.

4. Jean Haldane, *Religious Pilgrimage*. The Alban Institute, Mt. St. Alban, Washington, D.C., 1975. p. 20.

5. William Stringfellow, *A Public and Private Faith*. Eerdman's, Grand Rapids, 1962. p. 17.

6. Henri J. M. Nouwen, *Creative Ministry*. Doubleday, Garden City, 1971. p. 20.

7. Paul W. Hoon, *The Integrity of Worship*. Abingdon, Nashville, 1971. p. 9.

8. Ibid., p. 24.

9. William Abernathy, *A New Look for Sunday Morning*. Abingdon, Nashville, 1975. p. 173.

Chapter II

1. Hendrick Kraemer, *A Theology of the Laity.* Lutterworth Press, London, 1958. p. 132.
2. Henri Nouwen, *Reaching Out.* Doubleday, Garden City, 1975. p. 17.
3. Colin W. Williams, *What in the World.* National Council of Churches, 1964. p. 26.
4. Jeffrey Hadden, "Religion, Inc.," *Confusion and Hope.* Edited by Bucher and Hall. Fortress, Philadelphia, 1974. p. 13.
5. Sidney Skirven, "Christian Ministry in Earthen Vessels," Ibid. p. 46.

Chapter III

1. Michael Novak, *Ascent of the Mountain, Flight of the Dove.* Harper & Row, New York, 1971. p. 45.
2. The particular books referred to are:
John S. Dunne, *Time and Myth.* Doubleday, Garden City, 1973.
Robert P. Roth, *Story and Reality.* Eerdman's, Grand Rapids, 1973.
Sallie TeSelle, *Speaking in Parables.* Fortress Press, Philadelphia, 1975.
James William McLendon, Jr., *Biography as Theology.* Abingdon, Nashville, 1974.
Sam Keen, *To a Dancing God.* Harper & Row, New York, 1976.
Urban T. Holmes, III, *Ministry and Imagination.* Seabury, New York, 1976.
3. James B. Wiggins, ed., *Religion as Story.* Harper & Row, New York, 1975. p. 20.
4. John S. Dunne, *Time and Myth.* p. 1.
5. James William McLendon, Jr., *Biography as Theology.* p. 95.
6. Sidney Jourard, *The Transparent Self.* Van Nostrand, Princeton, 1964.
7. This was taken from a conference memo developed by the Adult Education Committee of St. John's Church, Georgetown Parish, 3240 O Street, Washington, D. C., 20007.
8. William Stringfellow, *A Private and Public Faith.* Eerdman's, Grand Rapids, 1962. pp. 54–55.

9. International Review of Mission, Vol. LXV, No. 257, January, 1976. p. 103.

10. Sheldon B. Kopp, *If You Meet the Buddha on the Road, Kill Him!* Ben Lomond, California, Science and Behavior Book, 1972. p. 14.

Chapter IV

1. Glen Richard Bucher and Patricia Ruth Hill (eds.), *Confusion and Hope.* Fortress Press, Philadelphia, 1974. p. 12.

2. John Howard Yoder, *The Politics of Jesus.* Eerdman's, Grand Rapids, 1972. pp. 147, 148.

3. Alvin Toffler, *Future Shock.* Bantam Books, New York, 1971. p. 17.

4. Robert M. Pirsig, *Zen and the Art of Motorcycle Maintenance.* Bantam Books, New York, 1975. pp. 163, 164.

5. Dietrich Bonhoeffer, *Letters and Papers from Prison.* Fontana Books, London, 1959. p. 161.

Chapter V

1. *The Church for Others.* World Council of Churches, Geneva, 1967. pp. 14, 15.

2. Markus Barth, *The Broken Wall.* Judson Press, Chicago, 1959. p. 43

3. James Wm. McClendon, Jr., *Biography as Theology.* Abingdon, Nashville, 1974. p. 63.

4. Metropolitan Associates of Philadelphia, *A Strategy of Hope.* Available through Department of Evangelism, American Baptist Churches, Valley Forge, PA.

5. I am indebted to my colleague, Dr. G. Douglass Lewis of the Hartford Seminary Foundation, for these elements in conflict management.

6. Donald A. McGavran and Winfield C. Arn, *How to Grow a Church.* G/L Publications, Glendale, CA, 1975. p. 4.

7. John S. Savage, The Apathetic and Bored Church Member: *Psychological and Theological Implications.* Lead Consultants, Pittsford, New York.

8. Henri Nouwen, *Reaching Out.* Doubleday, Garden City, 1974. p. 112.

Chapter VI

1. Bryan Hall, Director of the Center for Values and Meaning (CEVAM), Indianapolis, Indiana, in an address at Hartford Seminary Foundation, May 22, 1975.

2. Jacob Needleman and Dennis Lewis, *Sacred Tradition and Present Need.* Viking Press, New York, 1975. p. 7.

3. Henri Nouwen, *Reaching Out.* Doubleday, Garden City, 1974. p. 96.

4. Paul Tillich, *The Eternal Now.* Scribner, New York, 1963. p. 18.

5. Ira Progoff, *At a Journal Workshop.* Dialogue House Library, 1975.

6. Claudio Naranjo and Robert Ornstein, *On the Psychology of Meditation.* Viking Press, New York, 1971. p. 8.

7. Quoted in Ibid., p. 7.

8. Thomas Merton, *New Seeds of Contemplation.* New Directions, New York, 1961. p. 3.

9. Ibid., p. 56.

10. Ira Progoff, *The Well and the Cathedral.* Dialogue House Library, 1972.

11. Henri Nouwen, *The Wounded Healer.* Doubleday, Garden City, 1972. p. 67.

12. Pierre-Yves Emery, *Prayer at the Heart of Life.* Orbis, Maryknoll, New York. 1975. pp. 131, 132.

13. Thomas Merton, *Conjectures of a Guilty Bystander.* Image, 1968. p. 86.

14. Dag Hammarskjold, *Markings.* Alfred A. Knopf, 1964. p. 13.

Chapter VII

1. Peter Rudge, *Ministry and Management,* Tavistock, Barnes and Noble, 1968.

2. Henri J. M. Nouwen, *The Wounded Healer,* Doubleday, Garden City, 1972, p. 103.

3. Quoted from a paper, "Support Systems," written in 1974 by the Rt. Rev. David Richards and distributed by the Office of Pastoral Development, 116 Alhambra Circle, Coral Gables, Florida 33134.

Chapter VIII

1. James Wall, in an address given at The Hartford Seminary Foundation, June 9, 1976.

2. Genevieve Burch, *Continuing Professional Education Interests of Clergy* (Report of a Survey of Clergy of the Albany, New York area). Hartford Seminary Foundation, Hartford, CT, 1974. p. 18.

3. Ibid., p. 19.

Chapter IX

1. Robert L. Heilbroner, *An Inquiry into the Human Prospect.* W. W. Norton, New York, 1974. pp. 21, 137.

2. Thomas Merton, *New Seeds of Contemplation.* New Directions, New York, 1961. pp. 136, 106.

3. Leslie Newbegin, *Honest Religion for Secular Man.* Westminster, Philadelphia, 1966. p. 93.

4. Colin Williams in an address delivered at The Hartford Seminary Foundation, January, 1976.

5. Douglas John Hall, *The Reality of the Gospel and the Unreality of the Churches.* Westminister, Philadelphia, 1975. p. 130.

6. John Biersdorf, "New Wine in Old Skins, and Vice Versa," *Journal of Applied Behavior Science,* Vol. 9, 1973.

7. "Taking Charge," American Friends Service Committee, San Francisco, 1975.

8. Martin Marty, *Death and Birth of the Parish.* Concordia, St. Louis, 1964. pp. 12, 13.